Men-at-Arms • 542

Yugoslav Armies 1941–45

Nigel Thomas PhD • Illustrated by Johnny Shumate
& Dušan Babac

Series editors Martin Windrow & Nick Reynolds

OSPREY PUBLISHING
Bloomsbury Publishing Plc
Kemp House, Chawley Park, Cumnor Hill, Oxford OX2 9PH, UK
29 Earlsfort Terrace, Dublin 2, Ireland
1385 Broadway, 5th Floor, New York, NY 10018, USA
E-mail: info@ospreypublishing.com
www.ospreypublishing.com

OSPREY is a trademark of Osprey Publishing Ltd

First published in Great Britain in 2022

A catalogue record for this book is available from the British Library

ISBN: PB: 9781472842039; eBook:9781472842046;
ePDF:9781472842015; XML: 9781472842022

22 23 24 25 26   10 9 8 7 6 5 4 3 2 1

Editor: Martin Windrow
Map & Chart 1 by Darko Pavlović
Charts 2 & 3 by Nigel Thomas
Index by Zoe Ross
Typeset by PDQ Digital Media Solutions, Bungay, UK
Printed in India by Replika Press Private Ltd

MIX
Paper from
responsible sources
FSC® C016779
FSC
www.fsc.org

Osprey Publishing supports the Woodland Trust, the UK's leading woodland conservation charity.

To find out more about our authors and books, visit
www.ospreypublishing.com . Here you will find extracts, author interviews, details of forthcoming events, and the option to sign up for our newsletter.

OPPOSITE
A Chetnik machine-gunner in Lika, Western Croatia, carrying a 7.9mm M1937 Zbrojovka ('Zorka') LMG, a variant of the Czech ZB26 produced under licence at the Kragujevac arsenal. Note the *kalpak* cap, bandoliers with 5-round stripper clips of rifle ammunition, and M1935 fragmentation grenade. (Miloslav Samardžić 'Pogledi' Archive)

Dedication

Dušan Babac would like to dedicate this book to his late father, Marko Babac

Acknowledgements

Nigel Thomas would like to thank the correspondents whose interest, kindness and patience have contributed so much to this book: Barbara Allen, Christopher Harrod, Dr Marc Landry and Krunoslav Mikulan, as well as his wife Heather and sons Alexander and Dominick for their tireless encouragement and support. He also acknowledges the published work of Krunoslav Mikulan.
For further information on Nigel Thomas or to contact him please refer to his website: nt-associates.com.
Dušan Babac would like to thank Miloslav Samardžić, Čedomir Vasić, Ivona Fregl, Ratomir Milikić, Aleksandar Smiljanić and Bratislav Stanković, who generously shared information and photographs from their collections. He would also like to thank his wife Tatjana and his sons Vukašin, Rastko and Marko for their love and support.

Editor's note
To save space, this text departs from Osprey's usual house style, incorporating abbreviated dates and unit designations, and digits for numbers.

TITLE PAGE
In this group of Chetniks, *Narednik* (Sgt) of Gendarmerie Filip Ajdačić (2nd right), and his comrade (far right) wear the Yugoslav Army M1940 Assault Units' *kalpak* and M1939 NCOs' capbadge. All four sport beards – many Chetniks swore not to shave theirs off until final victory. Ajdačić carries a .45in M1928A1 Thompson SMG; promoted to *Poručnik* (Lt), he would command the Kosjerić Brigade. (Miloslav Samardžić 'Pogledi' Archive)

Abbreviations used in this text:

AA	anti-aircraft	LMG	light machine gun
AG	army group	Lt	light *or* lieutenant
Arty	artillery	Maj	major
AT	anti-tank	med	medical
Bde	brigade	MG	machine gun
Bn	battalion	Mot	motorized
Brig	brigadier	MT	motor transport
Bty/s	battery/ies	Mtn	mountain
Capt	captain	NCO	non-commissioned officer
Cav	cavalry	NDH	Independent State of Croatia (Axis- allied)
CDK	Montenegro Volunteer Corps (Chetnik)	NOPOJ, NOP i DVJ & NOV i POJ	Successive designations of Partisan army & detachments 1941–44
Co	company		
Cpl	corporal		
Det	detachment *(odred)*		
Div	division		
Eng	engineer	OC	officer commanding
Gen	general	Ptn	platoon
GHQ	general headquarters	Regt	regiment
GJK	group of shock corps (Chetnik)	SDS, SGS SUK	Gen Nedić's Serbian forces (Axis-allied 1941–44) Chetnik-allied 1944–45)
GK	group of corps (Chetnik)		
Grp	group		
GŠ	Partisan GHQ (later, VŠ)	Sgt	sergeant
HQ	headquarters	Sigs	signals
Inf	infantry	SMG	sub-machine gun
JA	Partisan army, 1945	Tspt	transport
JK	shock corps (Chetnik)	VK	Yugoslav GHQ, 1941
JV	pre-war Yugoslav Army	WO	warrant officer
JVuO	Chetnik army		

YUGOSLAV ARMIES 1941–45

INTRODUCTION

Birth of the Yugoslav state

As a political entity, Yugoslavia dated from 6 November 1817, when the south Slav principality of Serbia in the western Balkans, having broken away from the Ottoman Empire, was internationally recognized as an independent state. Subsequently, Serbia launched several campaigns of territorial expansion in attempts to unite all ethnic Serbs under one flag. It liberated most of Kosovo from Ottoman rule by June 1913, followed by Vardar Macedonia ('South Serbia'; today, Northern Macedonia) in August 1913, after the First and Second Balkan Wars respectively.

During World War I, Serbia and its ethnic-Serb neighbour Montenegro fought for the Entente against the Central Powers, though the latter also included south Slavs in six regions of the Austro–Hungarian Empire. On 29 October 1918 these regions (Slovenia, Croatia, Slavonia, Bosnia–Herzegovina, Syrmia and Dalmatia) declared independence as the 'State of the Slovenes, Croats and Serbs'. However, on 1 December 1918 Serbia absorbed this proto-state, and also the ethnic-Hungarian Vojvodina region (Banat, Bačka and Baranja). On 25 November 1918 an assembly of Serbs and other Slavs of Vojvodina proclaimed in Novi Sad the unification of Vojvodina with the Kingdom of Serbia, Montenegro and Prekmurje, as 'the Kingdom of the Serbs, Croats and Slovenes' (Kraljevina Srba, Hrvata i Slovenaca – SHS). On 9 January 1919 the SHS absorbed Medjumurje in northern Croatia, and on 27 November four Bulgarian border districts.

Inter-war developments

Despite the kingdom's title, it was effectively a 'Greater Serbia' under the Serbian Karagorgević royal house, with other ethnic groups – Croats, Slovenes, Albanians, Bosnian Moslems, Hungarians and Germans – permitted only limited political influence. Events were dominated by politico-religious rivalry between the Orthodox Serbs and Catholic Croats, compelling King Aleksandar I to rename the kingdom formed from these many communities as Yugoslavia (*Jugoslavija*) – 'Land of the Southern Slavs' – which he ruled as a dictator from 3 October 1929.

In that month Yugoslavia was reorganized administratively into Belgrade – the capital – and nine provinces (*Banovina*): Dravska (now Slovenia), Drinska (S Bosnia–Herzegovina), Dunavska (Vojvodina/ N Serbia), Moravska (Central Serbia), Primorska (Croatia–Dalmatia), Savska (Croatia–Slavonia), Vardarska (S Serbia–Macedonia), Vrbaska (N Bosnia–Herzegovina) and Zetska (Montenegro)[1].

Serbo–Croatian tensions persisted, and on 9 October 1934 King Aleksandar was assassinated in Marseilles by Vlado Chernozemski, a Bulgarian activist, supported by Croatian *Ustasha* terrorists. Aleksandar was succeeded by 11-year-old Prince Petar, with Aleksandar's cousin Prince Pavle ruling as regent until Petar's 18th birthday. In an attempt to appease the Croats, Yugoslav Prime Minister Dragiša Cvetkovič and Croatian political leader Vladko Maček signed an agreement on 24 August 1939, uniting Primorska and Savska provinces and neighbouring majority-Croat districts into the semi-autonomous Banovina of Hrvatska (Croatia).

Following the Franco–German Armistice of 22 June 1940, Yugoslavia, being militarily weak and almost entirely surrounded by hostile states, abandoned its traditional pro-British stance. On 25 March 1941 Prime Minister Cvetković signed the Axis Tripartite Pact with Germany, Italy and Japan – a deeply unpopular act, causing widespread riots in Serbian regions of Yugoslavia. Consequently, on 27 March *Brigadni djeneral* Borivoye Mirković, the Air Force commander, led a coup d'état, replacing Cvetković with *Armijski djeneral* Dušan Simović; installing the 17-year-old Prince Petar as King Petar II; cancelling the Tripartite Pact, and declaring for the Allies. Hitler, outraged at this defiance, activated on 6 April 1941 Operation '*25*', the invasion of Yugoslavia. Planned in detail since 1940, this assigned 22 German, Italian, Hungarian and Bulgarian divisions to a synchronized operation which was to take no more than ten days.

THE YUGOSLAV ARMY IN 1941

On Dec 1918 the Serbian Army became the Army of the Kingdom of the Serbs, Croats and Slovenes (*Vojska Kraljevine Srba, Hrvata i Slovenaca*). On 3 Oct 1929 it was renamed the Yugoslav Army (*Jugoslovenska Vojska* – JV), directed by the Supreme Command (*Vrhovna komanda* – VK).

Army Groups
The VK controlled an army-sized Strategic Reserve with HQ troops (inf regts; tank bn; arty bns; mot medium arty regts; mot AA bns; Army AA MG cos; mot eng regts); 4 inf divs in strategic reserve; and three army groups (*Grupa armija* – GAs). Each GA contained HQ troops (horse arty bns; Army arty regts; mot AA bns; Army AA MG cos; and tspt regts); and 2 Armies, totalling 4–8 divisions.

---

1   *Banovina*, divisional and detachment names in Serbo-Croat take the possessive case; e.g. *Zetska Banovina* (Zeta's Province), *Savska Divizija* (Sava's Division) or *Komski Odred* (Kom's Detachment).

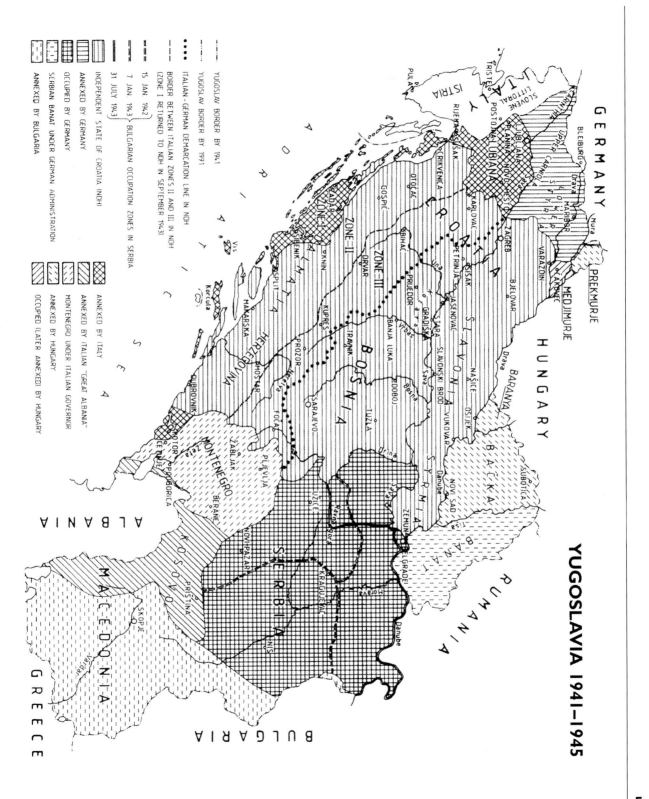

YUGOSLAVIA 1941–1945

Legend

- ------ YUGOSLAV BORDER BY 1941
- ------ YUGOSLAV BORDER BY 1991
- •••• BORDER BETWEEN ITALIAN ZONES II AND III IN NDH
- ——— ITALIAN-GERMAN DEMARCATION LINE IN NDH (ZONE I RETURNED TO NDH IN SEPTEMBER 1943)
- ———— BULGARIAN OCCUPATION ZONES IN SERBIA
  - 15 JAN. 1942
  - 7 JAN. 1943
  - 31 JULY 1943
- INDEPENDENT STATE OF CROATIA (NDH)
- ANNEXED BY GERMANY
- OCCUPIED BY GERMANY
- SERBIAN BANAT UNDER GERMAN ADMINISTRATION
- ANNEXED BY BULGARIA
- ANNEXED BY ITALY
- ANNEXED BY ITALIAN "GREAT ALBANIA"
- MONTENEGRO UNDER ITALIAN GOVERNOR
- ANNEXED BY HUNGARY
- OCCUPIED (LATER ANNEXED) BY HUNGARY

5

Table 1: Selected branch & unit distinctions, Yugoslav Army, April 1941

Branch and unit type	Branch colour	Button	Unit number or monogram, etc
General officers	Light blue	Gold	–
Brigadiers	Branch colour	Branch	–
General Staff officers	Light red	Gold	M1924 or M1939 aiguillettes
Royal Guard Cavalry Bde	Mid-blue	Silver	Crown, п /II / mid-blue L-shaped collar braid
Royal Guard Infantry Regt	Dark red	Gold	Crown, п /II / dark red L-shaped collar braid
Royal Guard Artillery Regt	Black	Gold	Crown, п /II / black L-shaped collar braid
12 named divisional Infantry Regts (a, opposite)	Dark red	Gold	1, 2, 5-8, 11, 14, 16, 25, 38, 54/ monogram
79 divisional Infantry Regts	Dark red	Gold	3, 4, 9, 10, 12, 13, 15, 17–24, 26–37, 39–51, 53, 55–66, 70, 72, 74–76, 83–85, 87, 89–92, 104–106, 108, 110, 112, 119, 121, 126, 128, 137, 150, 151
Šibenik Fort Command, 137 Inf Regt	Dark red	Gold	ш
Boka Kotor Fort Comd, 150 &151 Inf Regts	Dark red	Gold	B K
10 Divisional Machine–Gun Bns	Dark red	Gold	I – X
19 Divisional Machine–Gun Cos	Dark red	Gold	I – XIX
2 Mountain Infantry Regts	Dark red	Gold	1 – 2 / hunting horn
2 Motorcycle Bns	Dark red	Gold	2, 3 / winged wheel & steering wheel `
1 Mechanized Bn	Dark red	Gold	winged tyre on crossed rifles
1 Motorized Bn	Dark red	Gold	III / winged tyre on crossed swords
2 Bicycle Bns	Dark red	Gold	I – II / crossed point-down bayonets & wheel
2 GHQ Tank Bns	Black	Gold	I – II / tank
6 Army (Chetnik) Assault Bns	Black	Gold	1– 6 / skull & crossbones
17 Border Guard Infantry Bns	Dark red	Gold	I – VIII, X – XVIII / Edelweiß on collar
6 named divisional Cavalry Regts (b, opposite)	Dark-blue	Silver	3 – 8/ monogram
2 divisional Cavalry Regts	Dark-blue	Silver	1, 2
7 Army Cavalry Regts	Dark-blue	Silver	51, 56, 61, 66, 71, 76, 81
28 Cavalry Bns	Dark-blue	Silver	1, 3, 5, 7–10, 12, 13, 15, 17, 20, 22, 25, 27, 31–4, 38, 40, 42, 44, 46–9
5 GHQ Artillery Regts	Black	Gold	1 – 5 / crossed cannons
7 Army Artillery Regts	Black	Gold	51, 56, 66, 61, 71, 76, 81 /crossed cannons
1 named divisional Artillery Regt (c, opposite)	Black	Gold	30/ monogram
27 divisional Artillery Regts	Black	Gold	1, 3, 5, 7–10, 12, 13, 15, 17, 20, 22, 25, 27, 31–4, 38, 40, 42, 44, 46–9/ crossed cannons
24 Independent Artillery Bns	Black	Gold	1– 24 / crossed cannons
Fortress Artillery Regts	Black	Gold	Numbers / fortress
3 Motorized Heavy Artillery Regts	Black	Gold	113 – 115 / large grenade on large crossed cannons
2 Motorized Heavy Artillery Bns	Black	Gold	101, 102 / large grenade on large crossed cannons
2 Motorized Medium Artillery Regts	Black	Gold	101, 102 / large grenade on large crossed cannons
3 Horse Artillery Bns	Black	Gold	I – II1 / crossed cannon & sabre
2 Mountain Artillery Bns	Black	Gold	4 – 5 / hunting horn
2 Mountain Artillery Batteries	Black	Gold	1 – 2 / hunting horn
10 Motorized Anti-Aircraft Bns	Black	Gold	1– 10 / eagle on crossed cannons
6 Army Anti-Aircraft MG Cos	Black	Gold	1 – 6 / eagle on crossed cannons
15 Border Guard Artillery Bns	Black	Gold	I – XV / crossed cannons
2 Motorized Engineer Regts	Violet	Silver	1, 2 / crossed pickaxe & spade
7 Army Engineer Bns	Violet	Silver	51, 56, 61, 66, 71, 76, 81 / Crossed pickaxe & spade
28 divisional Engineer Bns	Violet	Silver	1 – 28 / crossed pickaxe & spade
14 Bridging Engineer Bns.	Violet	Silver	1– 14 / fouled anchor on crossed hammer & oar
2 Motorized Engineer Regts	Violet	Silver	1, 2 / fouled anchor on crossed hammer & oar
28 divisional Signals Cos.	Violet	Silver	1 – 28 / 2 lightning flashes
7 Army Transport Regts	Dark red	Gold	1– 6, 32 / winged wheel
Supply officers	Dark red	Gold	crossed swords on a basket of corn
Medical Corps	Brown	Silver	snake & staff
Veterinary Corps	Brown	Gold	horse's head, snake & staff
Military Officials (1939–1941)	Violet	Silver	–

Armies

There were 8 Army Districts, designated 1.–7. and Coastal. The Districts formed 5 Armies (1.– 4. & 7.), plus 3. Territorial Army *(3. Teritorialna armija)* formed from surplus District units allocated to the three Army Groups. There were also three independent Armies (5., 6. & Coastal). An Army comprised HQ troops (inf regts; tank bn; cav bde; cav regts/ bns; Army arty regts/ bns; heavy arty regts/ bns; Army AA bns; mot AA bns; Army AA MG cos; tspt regts); plus 1–4 inf divs, 1 cav div, and 1–4 detachments.

Divisions

There were 28 inf divisions. Each Army District *(Armijska oblast)* comprised 1–4 Divisional Recruiting Districts, totalling 16 peacetime inf divisions. A Divisional District *(Divizijska oblast)* raised one inf div bearing a 1–50 series number and the District name, which was usually a geographical feature, town or region. The 16 divs/districts were: 3. Dunavska; 5. Šumadiska; 7. Potiska; 9. Timočka; 10. Bosanska; 12. Jadranska; 15. Zetska; 17. Vrbaska; 20. Bregalnička; 25. Vardarska; 27. Savska; 30. Osiječka, 31. Kosovska; 38. Dravska; 46. Moravska, and 50. Drinska. A further 12 war-raised inf divs were formed from surplus troops across the Districts: 1. Cerska; 8. Krajinska; 13. Hercegovačka; 22. Ibarska; 32. Triglavska; 33. Lička; 34. Toplička; 40. Slavonska; 42. Murska; 44. Unska, 47. Dinarska and 49. Sremska. An inf div *(pešadijska divizija)* comprised HQ troops (AT and MG cos, eng bn, 3 mot tspt cos), plus 3 inf regts, an arty regt and a cav battalion. An inf regt comprised 3 bns, each with 4 companies.

The élite Royal Guards *(Kraljeva Garda)* were at divisional strength. They comprised an HQ; Guards Cav Bde (1–2 Guards Cav Regts); Guards Inf Regt; Guards Arty Regt (Horse Arty and Mtn Arty Bns, each with 2 btys); Eng and Mot Tspt Companies).

There were three cav divs, numbered 1.–3. A cav div *(konjička divizija)* had HQ troops (AT bn; eng, sigs, tspt and light bridging-train units); plus 2 cav bdes, each with 2 cav regts, each with 4 rifle and 1 MG sqns and a technical sqn (eng and sigs ptns); a bicycle bn, with 3 rifle and 1 MG cos; and an arty regt (horse arty bn with 2 field and 1 mtn batteries).

Brigades & Detachments

An Army Brigade *(brigada)* was a temporary pairing of 2 regts within a division. These were supplemented in 1941 by the Guards Cav Bde, a line

1935: *Kapetan I klase* **Pavle Babac, commanding 1st Company of 2nd 'Prince Mihailo' Infantry Regt – called 'the Iron Regiment' since a famous bayonet-charge against Bulgarian troops at Bregalnica on 18 June 1913, during the Second Balkan War. Compare with Plate A1, and Plate E1 for the 1930-pattern regimental flag in the background. (Dušan Babac Collection)**

Regimental monograms

(a) Infantry Regts:

Crown, MI = 1 Inf Regt Miloš the Great

Crown, MB = 2 Inf Regt Prince Michail

Crown, MI = 5 Inf Regt King Milan

Crown, AI = 6 Inf Regt Alexander I

Crown, п/I = 7 Inf Regt King Peter I

Crown, AI = 8 Inf Regt Alexander I

Crown, T/ п = 11 Inf Regt Karageorge

Crown, п/II = 14 Inf Regt King Petar II

Crown, H/II = 16 Inf Regt Nicholas II

Crown, FF = 25 Inf Regt King Ferdinand

Crown, FUUN = 38 Inf Regt Njegos

Crown, CC = 54 Inf Regt King Carol II

(b) Cavalry Regts:

Crown, M = 3 Cav Regt Queen Maria

Crown, K = 4 Regt Duke Konstantin

Crown, M = 5 Regt Queen Maria

Crown, A = 6 Regt Prince Arsenija

Crown, п = 7 Regt Prince Paul

Crown, A = 8 Regt Prince Andrew

(c) Artillery Regt:

Crown, T = 30 Arty Regt Tomislav

cav bde, and 2 fortress commands An independent cav bde was based
with 6. Army, and Šibenik and Boka Kotor Fortress Commands defended
Adriatic naval bases.

There were also 18 temporary brigade-status battle-groups called
'Detachments'. A Detachment (*Odred*) contained units – usually an inf
or cav regt and a field arty bn – detached from an inf or cav division.
They were designated as follows: Banatski, Braničevski, Čaplinski,
Kalinski, Komski, Lički, Ormoski, Požarevacki, Risnjacki, Savski, Secanski,
Smederevski, Somborski, Strumički, Trebinski, Triglavski, Vlasinski,
and Žabaljski.

UNIFORMS

The uniform colour since 1922 was greenish-grey (*sivo-maslinasta*). The
most recent Yugoslav Army infantry uniform was the M1939 (introduced
30 Aug 1939), although many troops wore older items. For branch and
button colours, and shoulder-strap insignia, see Table 1 on pages 6–7.

Cap insignia

M1922 cockade (introduced 2 Jan 1922). Officers wore an oval enamel
red (outer), blue (inner), white (central) cockade with a gold King
Aleksandar I monogram. The NCOs' cockade omitted the monogram,
and enlisted men wore no cockade.
M1934 cockade (introduced 9 Oct 1934). The monogram changed to
reflect the succession of King Petar II.
M1939 cap badge (introduced 30 Aug 1939). Officers wore a silver metal
double-headed eagle, gold wreath, crown and Petar II monogram, on
a branch-colour cloth backing. NCOs wore a silver metal shield with

the coat of arms of Serbia, Croatia and Slovenia, on a crowned double-headed eagle, on a branch-colour cloth backing. Enlisted men had no cap badge.

General officers' & officers' dress uniforms
The general officers' black M1935 dress uniform (introduced 16 Jan 1935) comprised a peaked cap (red for *armijski djeneral*); single-breasted 6-button tunic, with gold oakleaves on standing collar; black trousers, and gold braid belt. Other officers wore a branch-colour tunic with a plain branch-colour collar.

The general officers' mid-blue M1939 dress uniform included a peaked cap with a light blue band. The double-breasted 'lancer' tunic had 2 rows of 6 gold buttons bearing the double-headed eagle; gold oakleaves on a light blue standing collar; plaited gold braid shoulder straps on light-blue underlay; and deep turnback cuffs decorated with gold oakleaves. The rectangular, scalloped, vertical cuff patches had 3 buttons, and the collar, cuff, cuff-patches, front and bottom edges were piped light blue. The light blue trousers had bright red outseam-piping between 2 broad red stripes; the gold-braid belt was retained. The rank of *brigadni djeneral* wore a branch-colour uniform with cuff and collar braid; other officers, a branch-colour cap and tunic with a plain collar, no cuff patches, and sometimes contrasting coloured trousers.

Undress uniforms
Officers, warrant officers and NCOs had undress service uniforms. The M1922 summer uniform comprised a white peaked cap with white synthetic-leather chinstrap and peak; a plain white cotton M1922 tunic; greenish-grey breeches, and riding boots.

The officers' M1935 undress uniform was greenish-grey. It comprised a peaked cap; an M1935 *dolman* (patrol jacket) worn instead of the M1922 or M1939 service tunic (see below); breeches and riding boots, but no belt. The *dolman* had a fly front; branch-colour 'spearhead' collar patches with a button; branch-colour collar piping; shoulder straps; internal breast pockets with scalloped buttoned flaps; internal slash waist pockets without flaps, and deep, piped turnback cuffs. General officers had gold braid collar patches, and bright red lining visible when front buttons were left open.

The M1935 cavalry undress (introduced 16 Jan 1935) had a mid-blue M1922 peaked cap with dark blue band; a mid-blue tunic with standing gold-braid collar; 6 gold front buttons; internal breast pockets with buttonless scalloped flaps; gold piping to the front and bottom edges and the cuffs; red trousers with a broad dark blue outseam-stripe; and a silver braid belt with dark blue interwoven threads.

Service uniforms
The general officers' greenish-grey M1922 service uniform (introduced 2 Mar 1922) had a peaked *šajkača* cap with button-colour crown piping and

1934/35: *Potporučnik* (2nd Lt) Dušan Milikić of the Royal Guard Infantry in service uniform plus helmet and binoculars. He wears the Serbian-pattern M1922 Adrian helmet painted greenish-grey, with a Yugoslav frontal plate. The officers' tunic is closed with brass 'peg' (toggle) buttons, and the standing collar is almost hidden by large L-shaped braid patches of dark red infantry branch-colour. On his shoulder straps is King Petar's monogram, and on his left sleeve a black mourning band worn by officers for six months following the assassination of King Alexandar on 9 October 1934. (Courtesy Milikić family)

Infantry subaltern officer in field uniform with greatcoat, helmet, binoculars, mapcase, and officers' dagger – compare with Plate A1. Note his non-regulation low half-laced marching boots. (Dušan Babac Collection)

wide metallic braid edging, a cockade, and a black leather peak and chinstrap. The tunic had a light blue (*brigadni djeneral*, branch-colour) standing collar; shoulder straps; fly front; external breast pockets and internal waist pockets with scalloped flaps; and piped turnback cuffs. The riding breeches had two broad red stripes. The brown M1935 waist belt had a cross-brace over the right shoulder, 'Sam Browne' style.

Field officers lacked the wide field-cap braid and the breeches stripes; and subaltern and warrant officers had branch-colour cap crown piping. They wore a peaked *šajkača* fieldcap, branch-colour collar patches and shoulder straps, and the brown belt with cross-brace.

Enlisted men wore a peakless M1922 or M1924 (1cm lower) field cap. Their M1924 greenish-grey double-breasted *koporan* tunic had large branch-colour collar patches; rectangular shoulder straps; plain cuffs; a fly front; and internal waist pockets with rectangular buttonless flaps. Greenish-grey breeches were worn with cloth puttees and brown ankle boots.

The general officers' greenish-grey double-breasted M1922 greatcoat had a turn-down collar with gold-braid 'spearhead' patches with gold buttons; shoulder straps of rank; 2 rows of 6 front buttons; light blue front lining, and light blue edge-piping to the front, cuffs, and squared flaps of the internal waist pockets. A horizontal rear half-belt had 2 gold buttons, and 2 vertical extensions with buttons and branch-colour piping. The 'Sam Browne' belt was worn over the greatcoat. The greatcoats of other officers and warrant officers had branch-colour piping and plain front lining. Those of NCOs and enlisted men had branch-colour rhomboid collar patches, rectangular shoulder straps, and no piping.

The M1939 service uniform was identical to the M1922, except that the *šajkača* had no peak or chinstrap, and the capbadge was an eagle and royal monogram (see text page 8). Officers and warrant officers retained the M1922 summer uniform, while enlisted men wore a white cotton M1939 tunic with M1939 greenish-grey *šajkača*, breeches and puttees.

Field uniforms

The M1922 field uniform was identical to the service uniform but could be worn with a steel helmet – an M1922 French Adrian painted greenish-grey with a Yugoslav eagle-and-shield frontal plate; an M1916 German; or an M1934 Czechoslovak *Čačak* without insignia (named after the Serbian town of manufacture). Officers and warrant officers wore a holstered Yugoslav-made .32in M1922 FN Browning pistol on the right hip, and on the left a binoculars case, officers with an M1939 dress dagger suspended below it. The M1922 service greatcoat was also worn.

Enlisted men wore an M1935 brown leather waistbelt and two M1924 Mauser ammunition pouches; a greenish-grey cloth M1924 backpack; an M1924 waterbottle on the right hip; an M1927 gasmask in a khaki webbing bag behind the right hip; and an M1924 general-purpose 'breadbag' haversack behind the left hip. The bayonet, in a black-painted scabbard, hung in a brown leather frog at the left hip.

The M1939 field uniform was similar to the M1922 except for the M1939 peakless field cap and M1927 Adrian helmet, and the M1933 Yugoslav *Obilićevo* gasmask in a cylindrical container. The officers' M1935 *dolman* might replace the field tunic. Enlisted men wore the M1939 greenish-grey field tunic with large branch-colour patches on the standing collar; pointed shoulder straps; a fly front; plain cuffs; and internal breast and waist pockets with scalloped buttonless flaps.

BRANCH-SPECIFIC ITEMS

Royal Guard

In dress uniform the Royal Guard cavalry wore red riding breeches with yellow outseam-piping, and black riding boots with gold top edging and rosettes. The officers' M1933 dress uniform comprised a black astrakhan fleece cap with a red bag, gold wire cap-lines, red crown, white heron-feather plume, and royal monogram. A dark green *Attila* shell-jacket was worn with gold chest, cuff, collar and lap braids, and a gold braid belt with cross-brace. Undress uniform included a light blue peaked cap with dark blue band- and crown-piping. A light blue hussar *pelisse* jacket had internal breast pockets with scalloped flaps; black fleece trim at the collar, cuffs, slash waist pockets, front and bottom edges; and gold collar and cuff embroidery. Enlisted men wore a black astrakhan *kalpak*, and a dark-green tunic with yellow braid trim.

The service uniform comprised a greenish-grey peaked cap with blue crown- and band-piping; a greenish-grey tunic with mid-blue L-shaped collar braids; narrow gold braid shoulder straps; double olive cord collar and front-piping, and Hungarian cuff-knots. Six brass 'pegs' (toggles) replaced buttons on the front and shoulder straps. Royal Guard infantry officers' M1924/M1937 dress uniform comprised a black astrakhan *kalpak* with a royal monogram, but without cap-lines or bag; a dark blue 6-toggle tunic with a standing gold braid collar, gold front and bottom edge-piping, and gold Hungarian cuff-knots; red breeches, and riding boots. The M1924 dark blue *milanka* undress comprised a dark blue peaked cap with red band and royal monogram; a dark blue *pelisse;* a gold braid belt; and red breeches with gold outseam-piping. The summer uniform, worn 1 May–15 Oct, was the service tunic in white cotton. The service tunic was identical to that of the Guard Cavalry but with dark red L-shaped collar braids.

The M1924/M1937 dress uniform of Royal Guard artillery officers comprised an astrakhan cap and a brown cloth infantry tunic; enlisted men wore yellow trim. The M1924 *milanka* undress uniform was dark brown, with cavalry breeches. The service tunic had black L-shaped collar braids.

Mountain Infantry

The 1st Mountain Inf Regt was formed 1 Aug 1931, and the M1932 greenish-grey uniform was introduced 4 Aug 1932. Officers wore *šajkača* caps with a cockade. The tunic had a turn-down collar with dark red L-shaped braids bearing silver sub-unit numbers (removed in wartime); 6

An infantryman wearing the M1939 uniform with field equipment, carrying his greatcoat in a 'horseshoe' roll – otherwise, compare with Plate A3. His weapon is the new M24 Mauser rifle produced under licence at the Kragujevac arsenal. (Dušan Babac Collection)

front buttons; 4 external pleated pockets with buttoned scalloped flaps; plain cuffs with horizontal buttoned flaps; and at the back, a vertical 'bellows' vent and a 2-button half-belt. M1932 'plus-four' trousers were worn with cloth puttees, and thick white socks folded down over brown mountain boots. The triangular enamel Mountain badge was worn above the right breast pocket. Officers wore gold braid rank bars on a uniform-colour patch piped dark red, on both sleeves above the cuffs, while WOs' patches were unpiped; NCOs had yellow upper-sleeve chevrons, points-up. A reinforced mountain cloak bore 'spearhead' collar patches, and rank bars on a chest patch.

The officers' and WOs' M1939 uniform had a turn-down collar with long branch-colour patches (buttonless 'spearhead' patches for enlisted men), and infantry rank shoulder straps. The Mountain Artillery branch-colour was black.

In April 1941 both Mountain detachments were deployed in the Slovenian Alps.

Tanks
In 1940 the Yugoslav Army purchased French Renault R35 light tanks: 1st Tank Bn had 54, and 2nd Bn received 45. The Cavalry School had 8 Czechoslovak Škoda Š-I-d T-32 tankettes, armoured lorries, and French Berliet-White and Italian SPA armoured cars. Tank crews wore a French M1919 helmet, with a light grey cotton summer overall and a brown leather M1935 jacket.

Kapetan I klase **Pavle Babac, now serving with 1st Mountain Inf Regt, wears the M1932 Mountain Inf officers' tunic with dark red L-shaped braids on the turn-down collar; the silver Roman numeral 'I' indicates a non-battalion sub-unit, here the regimental reconnaissance company. The officers' Mountain tunic had gold buttons bearing the *Edelweiß* badge, and (not visible here) rank bars above the cuffs. Note the triangular Mountain Troops' badge above his right pocket. (Dušan Babac Collection)**

Chetnik Assault Troops
Chetniks were Serbian guerrillas who formed bands in the 19th century to protect Serbian civilians under Ottoman occupation. The Chetnik Association was established in 1921, recruiting Great War veterans to preserve Chetnik traditions. The Chetnik Assault Troops (*Četničke (jurišne) trupe*) were formed on 24 Apr 1940 as élite deep-penetration light infantry units.

The uniform was worn with an officers' black astrakhan or enlisted men's sheepskin *kalpak* with a black cloth bag and tassel, or a *šajkača* cap. The greenish-grey M1940 'assault tunic' resembled the M1932 Mountain type, but had silver skull-and-crossbones badges on black collar patches, black collar- and cuff-flap piping, but standard shoulder straps. The 'assault cape' bore tunic collar patches, and a patch with rank bars on the left breast. The uniform was completed with baggy mountain trousers, puttees and climbing boots.

Border Guards
Border Guard infantry and artillery (formed 11 May 1940) wore standard M1939 uniforms, with M1940 silver *Edelweiß* flower badges on infantry dark red or artillery black collar patches. The M1940 NCO capbadge showed a silver metal crowned eagle and coats of arms on red enamel edged silver.

Rank titles & service-uniform insignia
(see Chart 1, page 29)
All branches used the same rank titles except for non-combat general officers, e.g., *sanitetski djeneral* (Medical Corps MajGen). Officers' rank titles were commonly prefixed by the appropriate branch.

- Field-marshal *(Vojvoda):* silver double-headed eagle on large (13cm x 5.5cm) gold-wire plaited shoulder straps on light blue underlay. The rank was introduced 20 Oct 1912 for exceptional merit in wartime, and by 1939 was only held on a non-active basis by FM Petar Bojović.
- General officers *(djenerali)*, from *armijski djeneral* to *brigadni djeneral:* from 9 Aug 1923, 13cm x 5.5cm button-colour wire plaited shoulder straps on light blue *(brigadni djeneral,* branch-colour) underlay; 3-1 gold metal 6-point sleeve stars. In May 1939 insignia changed to 3-1 button-colour metal shoulder-strap stars, but in Dec 1939 the M1923 sleeve insignia were readopted.
- Field officers *(viši oficiri)*, from *pukovnik* to *major:* unit numbers, branch badges or unit monograms, and 3-1 reverse button-colour 4-point stars, on narrower (13cm x 4.5cm) flat button-colour braid (or gilt brass) shoulder straps, with branch-colour edge-piping.
- Subaltern officers *(niši oficiri)*, from *kapetan I klase* to *potporučnik:* unit numbers, branch badges or unit monograms, and 4-1 reverse button-colour 4-point stars, on 13cm x 4.5cm flat button-colour braid shoulder straps, with branch-colour edge-piping and centre-stripe.
- Warrant officers *(podoficiri)*, from *narednik vodnik I* to *III klase* (introduced 9 Aug 1923). On service uniform, brass unit numbers, branch badges or monograms, 3-1 transverse button-colour braid bars, and 4 button-colour stars, on 13cm x 4.5cm branch-colour shoulder straps. From 1939 on field uniform, greenish-grey cloth shoulder straps with branch-colour piping, button-colour Arabic or Latin unit numbers, branch badges or monograms, and 4 stars.
- Non-commissioned officers (also *podoficiri)*, from *narednik* to *podnarednik:* pointed greenish-grey shoulder straps (branch-colour edge-piping for *narednik)*, with gold or silver metal Arabic or Latin unit numbers, branch badges or monograms, and 3-2 stars.
- Enlisted men *(redovi)*, *kaplar* and *redov:* pointed shoulder straps with gold or silver metal Arabic or Latin unit numbers, branch badges or monograms *(kaplar,* with 1 star).

In wartime, field uniform shoulder straps omitted unit numbers for security reasons.

Rank insignia patches
Gold braid rank bars were worn on a greenish-grey cloth rectangle on the left breast of the M1922 officers' raincoat or cape. General officers showed gold metal crossed swords above 3-1 narrow bars; field officers, 3-1 narrow bars above a medium bar; and subaltern officers, 4-1 narrow bars.

A *Major* of Chetnik Assault Troops in that branch's M1940 uniform. The officers' black astrakhan cap has a tasselled black bag falling on the right side. The tunic was similar to that of the Mountain Troops, with a turn-down collar, visible buttons, four patch pockets, and buttoned horizontal cuff-flaps. The black collar patches bear the skull-and-crossbones badge of this branch, and rank is displayed on the shoulder straps. (Bratislav Stankovic Collection)

An officer commanding a T-32 Škoda tankette, wearing tank overalls with the Adrian M1919 modified helmet for tank crews (see Plate D1). Eight T-32s were purchased from Czechoslovakia in 1937, and formed the Tank Sqn at the Cavalry School in Zemun, near Belgrade. They were painted in the camouflage colours of the 'Little Entente' (Yugoslavia, Czechoslovakia and Romania): dark green, ochre and chocolate-brown. Note the 7.9mm M1937 Zbrojovka LMG mounted on the turret. (Dušan Babac Collection)

The Mountain Troops' M1932 service tunic displayed rank insignia on greenish-grey rectangular patches on both lower sleeves above the cuffs. Officers wore M1932 gold braid rank bars, on patches piped in infantry dark red or artillery black; field officers displayed 3-1 medium bars, and subaltern officers 4-1 narrow bars. Warrant officers wore 3-1 narrow yellow bars on patches without piping. Shoulder straps and standard insignia were introduced in 1939, but M1932 rank patches continued to be worn on the left breast of the rainproof hooded cape. These bore black cloth rank bars: WOs, 3-1 narrow bars above a medium bar; NCOs, narrow bars only.

Tank troops displayed M1932 rank patches with dark red piping above the left breast pocket of their winter and summer overalls.

THE APRIL WAR, 6–18 April, 1941

Order of battle & anticipated plans
(see also Table 2, page 16)

The Yugoslav High Command expected German attacks from Austrian, Romanian and Bulgarian territory, supported by Hungarian forces from Hungary, and Italian divisions in Istria and Albania. The General Staff planned an organized retreat from the borders, followed by guerrilla warfare in the almost impenetrable Bosnian mountains. However, the Yugoslav government insisted on a defence of all borders, leaving a strategic reserve in Sarajevo, Bosnia. Meanwhile, Yugoslav 3 Army Group would neutralize Italian 9. Army in Albania before carrying out a fighting retreat through Vardar Macedonia, to join Greek and British allies in northern Greece.

The main Yugoslav field force comprised three Army Groups and two independent commands:

1 AG (*Armijski djeneral* **Milorad Petrović**) defended the Northern Front with 5 divs and 4 detachments. 7. Army would protect Slovenia from

German 7. Army in Germany and Italian 2. Army in Istria, while 4. Army defended Croatia-Slavonia from Hungarian 7. Army. This AG planned to check the German and Italian advance before withdrawing into Bosnia.

2 AG (*Armijski djeneral* **Milutin Nedić**) would fight on the Eastern Front along the Dunavska border, with 4 divs and 3 detachments. 2. Army would confront Hungarian 2. Army, while 1. Army guarded Vojvodina and Serbia from German 1. Army. This AG would also block attacks from Hungarian 2. Army or German 12. Army in Romania, before retreating into Serbia and Bosnia.

3 AG (*Armijski djeneral* **Milan Nedić**) had 14 divs and 9 detachments, to defend the Southern and South-Eastern Fronts. In the South, 3. Army guarded Montenegro and western Vardar Macedonia from Italian 9. Army in Albania, while 3. Territorial Army protected Vardar Macedonia from German 12. Army. In the South-East, 5. and 6. Army defended Vojvodina and Serbia, again against German 12. Army. The AG would neutralize the Italians in Albania before retreating through Vardar Macedonia, linking up with Greek and British allied forces in northern Greece.

Coastal Independent Army would defend the Adriatic coast from German and Italian naval forces with 1 div, 2 detachments, and 2 fortress commands.

GHQ Strategic Reserve, with 4 inf divs, stood ready in Sarajevo to deploy to any part of the country.

In the following account, towns are located with reference to present-day republics, not the 1939 *Banovinas*.

Campaigns: Northern Front

7 Apr: Germans advanced through Slovenia, breaching the Rupnik Line and defeating Dravska Div. *8 Apr:* Slovenia was occupied; troops from the Slovene Triglavska and Croatian Slavonska and Savska Divs deserted. *9 Apr:* Germans entered Croatia and occupied Zagreb, destroying Slavonska Div. *10 Apr:* Germans crossed from Hungary into Croatia, occupying Varaždin. *11 Apr:* Germans took Celje (Slovenia), Karlovac and Osijek (Croatia); Italians captured Ljubljana (Slovenia). *13 Apr:* Italians occupied Istria (Croatia). *14 Apr:* Germans captured Valjevo and Kraljevo (Serbia); Italians defeated Jadranska Div at Knin (Croatia). Axis forces now controlled most major towns, while Hungarians took Vojvodina. *16 Apr:* Italians occupied Metković (Croatia), and Sarajevo and Mostar (Bosnia–Herzegovina). *17 Apr:* Italians took Trebinje (Bosnia-Herzegovina), Dubrovnik (Croatia) and Slovenia. *18 Apr:* Yugoslav Army surrendered.

Soldiers of a Motorized Artillery battalion seated in an Austrian Steyr 640 (6x4) 2.5-ton all-terrain truck, towing a Czechoslovak Škoda 47mm VZ KPÚV 38 anti-tank gun. Note that the men are wearing the licence-made Czechoslovak Čačak helmets issued to some élite units. (Belgrade City Library)

Table 2: Yugoslav Army order of battle: April 1941

GHQ Reserve (Belgrade): 22, 37, 47, 48 Inf Regts.
- Strategic Reserve: 1. Cerska Inf Div (6, 27, 66 Inf Regts; 1 Arty Regt); 33. Lička Inf Div (44, 91, 106 Inf Regts; 33 Arty Regt); 44. Unska Inf Div, Bihac (26, 55, 121 Inf Regts; 44 Arty Regt); 47. Dinarska Inf Div (13, 84, 119 Inf Regts; 47 Cav Bn; 47 Arty Regt); 22, 37, 47, 48 Inf Regts; II Tank Bn; 9, 10 Mot AA Bns; 111, 112 Mot Medium Arty Regts; 1 & 2 Mot Eng Regts; 5 x Army AA MG Cos; 15 x independent Arty Bns.
- Coastal Independent Army (Kotor): 12. Jadranska Inf Div, Mostar (11, 54, 83 Inf Regts; 12 Arty Regt); Šibenik Fortress Command (137 Inf Regt; Indep Arty Bn); Boka Kotor Fortress Command (150, 151 Inf Regts; Arty Rgt): Eng Bn; Telegraph Co); Čaplinski Detachment, Čaplina (85 Inf Regt; I/13 Arty Bn); Trebinje Detachment, Trebinje (1 x Horse Arty Bn)

1. Army Group (Zagreb); Army Group HQ Reserve: 1 x Horse Arty Bn.
- 4. Army (Zagreb): 27. Savska Inf Div, Zagreb (35, 53, 104 Inf Regts; 27 Arty Regt); 40. Slavonska Inf Div, Slavonski Brod (42, 43, 108 Inf Regts; 27 Cav Bn; 40 Arty Regt); 42 Murska Inf Div, Varaždin (36, 105, 126 Inf Regts; 42 Arty Regt); Ormoski Detachment (39 Inf Regt; 6 Cav Regt; 1 Bicycle Bn); 127 Inf Regt; 81 Cav Regt; 47 Cav Bn; 81 Army Arty Regt; 4 Mot AA Bn; 4 Army AA MG Co; 4 Tspt Regt.
- 7. Army (Ljubljana): 32. Triglavska Inf Div, Celje (39, 40, 110 Inf Regts; 32 Arty Regt); 38. Dravska Inf Div, Ljubljana (45, 112, 128 Inf Regts; 38 Arty Regt); 1. Cav Div (2, 8 Cav Regts; 1 Horse Arty Bn); Lička Detachment, Planina (44 Inf Regt; I/17 Arty Bn); Risnjački Mount Detachment, Ribnica (2 Mtn Inf Regt with 11–13 Mtn Bns & 5 Mtn Arty Bty); Triglavski Mtn Detachment, Bistrica (1 Mtn Inf Regt; 4 Mtn Arty Bty); 71 Army Arty Regt; 7 Mot AA Bn.

2. Army Group (Sremska Mitrovica)
- 1. Army (Novi Sad): 7. Potiska Inf Div, Subotica (25, 34, 51 Inf Regts; 7 Cav Bn; I/7 Arty Bn); 3. Cav Div (3, 51, 66 Cav Regts; 3 Horse Arty Bn; 3 Mot Bn; 3 Motorcycle Bn); Secanski Detachment (56 Cav Regt, II/25 Arty Bn); Somborski Detachment (51 Inf Regt; 7 Cav Bn; 51 Army Arty Regt); Žabalski Detachment (7 Inf Regt; I/7 Arty Bn); 56 Army Arty Regt; 1 Mot AA Bn; 1 Army AA MG Co; 1 Tspt Regt.
- 2. Army (Sarajevo): 10. Bosanska Inf Div, Sarajevo (10, 15, 60 Inf Regts; 10 Arty Regt); 17. Vrbaska Inf Div, Banja Luka (33, 89, 90 Inf Regts; I/17 Arty Bn); 30. Osijek Inf Div, Osijek (17, 41, 64 Inf Regts; 30 Arty Regt); 76 Cav Regt; 76 Army Arty Regt; 2 Mot AA Bn; 2 Army AA MG Co; 2 Tspt Regt.

3. Army Group (Skopje): Army Group HQ Reserve: 22 Ibar Inf Div (4, 24, 58 Inf Regts; II/22 Arty Bn)
- 3. Army: 13. Hercegovačka Inf Div, Hercegnovi (29, 32, 85 Inf Regts; I/13 Arty Bn); 15. Zetska Inf Div, Cetinje (38, 61, 87 Inf Regts); 25. Vardarska Inf Div, Podgorica (21, 46, 50 Inf Regts; II/25 Arty Bn); 31. Kosovska Inf Div, Pristina (30, 31, 56 Inf Regts; 31 Arty Regt); Komski Cav Detachment (48 Inf Regt; II/22 Arty Bn); 66 Army Arty Bn; 3 Mot AA Bn; 3 Army AA MG Co; 3 Tspt Regt.
- 3. Territorial Army: 5. Šumadijska Inf Div, Kragujevac (19, 59, 72 Inf Regts; 5 Arty Regt); 20. Bregalnica Inf Div, Štip (23, 28, 40 Inf Regts; II/20 Arty Bn); 46. Moravska Inf Div, Niš (1, 62, 92 Inf Regts; 46 Arty Regt); Strumički Detachment (49 Inf Regt; II/20 Arty Bn); 21 Inf Regt; I Tank Bn; 114 Mot Heavy Arty Regt.

5 Independent Army: 8. Krajina Inf Div (9, 74, 76 Inf Regts; 8 Arty Regt); 9. Timočka Inf Div, Zajecar (14, 20, 75 Inf Regts; II/9 Arty Bn); 34. Toplica Inf Div, Toplica (3, 12, 16 Inf Regts; I/61 Arty Bn); 50. Drinska Inf Div, Valjevo (5, 63, 65 Inf Regts); 2. Cav Div (1, 7 Cav Regts; 2 Horse Arty Bn; II Bicycle Bn; 2 Motorcycle Bn); Kalinski Detachment (14 Inf Regt; II/9 Arty Bn); Vlasinski Detachment (1, 62 Inf Regts; 61 Cav Regt; 61 Army Arty Regt); 113 Mot Heavy Arty Regt; 5 Mot AA Bn; 5 Army AA MG Co; 5 Tspt Regt.

6 Independent Army (Belgrade): Guards Eng & Automobile Cos; 3. Dunavska Inf Div, Belgrade (19, 59, 72 Inf Regts; 3 Arty Regt); 49. Sremska Inf Div, Sremska Mitrovica (2, 7, 70 Inf Regts; 49 Arty Regt); Braničevski Detachment; Požarevačka Detachment; Smederevski Detachment; Banatski Detachment (Guards Cav Bde; 8 Inf Regt; 4 Cav Regt; I/49 Arty Bn); Savski Detachment (Guards Inf Regt; Guards Art Regt with Horse Arty Bn – 2 btys; Mount Arty Bn – 2 btys); 101,102 Mot Heavy Arty Bns; Cav Bde (5, 71 Cav Regts); 6 Mot AA Bn; 6 Tspt Regt.

Eastern Front

11 Apr: Germans from Romania occupied Kragujevac and Pančevo (Serbia), and Hungarians captured Baranja and Bačka districts (Vojvodina). *12 Apr:* Germans captured Belgrade, and Hungarians took Novi Sad (Vojvodina).

Southern Front

7 Apr: 3. Army in Montenegro entered Albania; Germans defeated Ibarska, Moravska and Bregalnička Divs in Vardar Macedonia. *8 Apr:* Zetska, Vardarska and Kosovska Divs entered Albania; Germans entered Vardar Macedonia from Bulgaria, occupying Pirot and destroying Toplička Div. *9 Apr:* Germans occupied Bitola (Vardar Macedonia). Vardarska Div surrendered to Germans and Italians, while Zetska fought on in Albania. Meanwhile German forces entered Yugoslav Banat from Romania, and occupied Niš (Serbia). *11 Apr:* Germans captured Vardarska and Šumadijska Divs, but Zetska and Kosovska Divs fought on in Albania. *12 Apr:* Germans took Prizren (Kosovo). *15 Apr:* Germans occupied Užice (Serbia) and captured the Yugoslav Supreme Command at Zvornik, near Sarajevo (Bosnia-Herzegovina). Toplička Div was destroyed at Sokobanja (Serbia), and Italians drove Zetska and Hercegnovčka Divs from Albania.

Coastal Front

9 Apr: Jadranska Div attacked Zara (Zadar, Croatia). *13 Apr:* Italians broke Jadranska Div's siege and occupied coastal towns and offshore islands. Zetska Div engaged Italian tanks. *15 Apr:* Italians occupied Split and Šibenik (Croatia) and the Adriatic coast.

Surrender

The 1.5 million-strong Yugoslav Armed Forces were defeated for three reasons. Firstly, they could not defend their long borders, only partly protected by modern defences. Secondly, their weapons, equipment and training were inadequate to engage the modern mechanized Wehrmacht. Thirdly, Yugoslavia was politically fragmented, with only the Serbs pro-Yugoslav; other nationalities, especially the Croats and Slovenes, were anti-Yugoslav, leading to many desertions. On 17 Apr 1941, Yugoslav Foreign Minister Aleksandar Cincar-Marković and Deputy Chief of General Staff *Divizijski djeneral* Radivoje Janković signed the surrender.

Yugoslavia was then dismembered by the Axis powers (see map, and also a more detailed account in MAA 282, *Axis Forces in Yugoslavia 1941–45*). Germany, Italy, Hungary and Bulgaria annexed or occupied much of its territory. The Independent State of Croatia (NDH) joined them under the *Ustasha* regime of Ante Pavelić, and Gen Milutin Nedić also established a puppet government in German-occupied Serbia.

ROYAL YUGOSLAV FORCES IN THE MIDDLE EAST, 1941–45

King Petar left Yugoslavia on 14 Apr 1941, and on 21 June established the Yugoslav government-in-exile in London, with Gen Simović as prime minister.

Royal Guards Battalion

The Royal Yugoslav Forces were formed in Cairo, British-occupied Egypt, in June 1941, with *Armijski djeneral* Bogoljub Ilić as Chief of Staff. Ilić formed the 1st Bn of Royal Yugoslav Guards at Camp El-Agamy, Alexandria (later, simply Royal Yugoslav Guards Bn; others were planned, but never formed). The unit numbered 530 men in an HQ and A-D Cos; it included Serb and Slovene officers, Yugoslav refugees, and local Yugoslav residents, plus 259 Slovene and Croat POWs from the Italian Army. The first OCs were *Major* Živan Knežević, and from Jan 1942 *Potpukovnik* Miloje Dinić.

On 19 Feb 1942, *Potpukovnik* Milan Prosen assumed command, and intensified training. On 4 Mar, after Rommel's second offensive reached the Gazala line, the Bn was ordered to Tobruk to relieve the Czechoslovak Battalion. Heading by lorry to 'Kennel's Box' south of Sidi Barrani, on 15 Mar it was diverted south into the Libyan desert to join 11 Indian Inf Bde, 4 Indian Div of British 8 Army. The Bn retreated on 23 Mar via Halfaya Pass, Sollum, and Mersa Matruh, reaching Cairo on 31 March. On 4 May it moved to El Dabaa to guard RAF airfields, then on 23 June to Atata near Haifa, Palestine, under British 9 Army, to guard an oil refinery.

During Jan–July 1942 Yugoslav officers loyal to *Brigadni djeneral* Borivoje Mirković intrigued against the 'Majors' League' of more junior officers for control of the Yugoslav forces. The latter prevailed, but the British lost patience with the Yugoslavs, vetoing the formation of further units. The Mirković faction transferred to British Army command and expanded to form the 800-strong 244 (Temporary) Bn, King's Own Royal Regt, based near Torah, Egypt, but this reverted in Nov 1942 to the Royal Yugoslav Guards Bn under *Potpukovnik* Prosen. From Dec 1942 Prosen headed a Yugoslav military mission in Algiers, where he recruited some 2,200 Slovenes and Croats from Italian Army POWs. The British, who were then shifting their support from the royalist guerrilla leader Mihailović to the Communist Partisan leader Tito, refused these troops passage to Cairo to join the Guards Bn, and in Oct 1943 formed them into three Yugoslav labour companies (numbered 386–388) of the British Auxiliary Military Pioneer Corps.

Palestine, 1942: warrant officer of 1st Bn, Royal Yugoslav Guards carrying the M1930 regimental flag. He wears British khaki battledress uniform; the fact that his rank of *narednik-vodnik I klase* is indicated by a British brass crown above two gold-braid bars on both lower sleeves suggests that the photo was taken following the regulations of 8 August 1942. A khaki arc-shaped title with 'YUGOSLAVIA' embroidered in red is also displayed at the top of both sleeves. (Dušan Babac Collection)

Meanwhile, on 1 Jan 1943 *Potpukovnik* Franc Stropnik assumed command of the Royal Guards Bn in Palestine, and in June 1943 it joined 25 Indian Inf Bde, 10 Indian Division. Partisan propaganda teams were undermining morale, however, and in Dec 1943 troops began to mutiny, some demanding transfer to Partisan overseas brigades then forming in southern Italy (see below, 'Overseas brigades'). Eventually, in Mar 1944 the Guards Bn, reduced to company size, was disbanded. In all some 1,200 men transferred to the Partisans in May 1944, many to 4 Tank Battalion. On 7 Mar 1945 the remaining personnel became refugees, or transferred to the Partisans.

Uniforms & insignia
(see also under Plate D)
Personnel in the Middle East adopted the British peaked khaki service cap with a silver two-headed eagle badge, service uniform, greatcoat, battledress, and tropical khaki drill (KD) uniform, while retaining the greenish-grey *šajkača* field cap.

First-pattern rank insignia (June 1941–8 Aug 1942) Gen Ilić wore an M1939 officers' capbadge, with a white eagle and gold royal monogram in a gold wreath, on a circular red cloth backing; gold wire plaited shoulder straps on red cloth underlay; and British general officers' red gorget patches. Other officers wore the capbadge on branch-colour backing, pre-1941 shoulder straps with 4-point stars, and branch-colour pentagonal collar patches. while Warrant officers and NCOs wore an M1939 silver eagle and monogram badge on branch-colour backing on British peaked caps. Warrant officers wore 3-1 gold braid bars on black underlay, and NCOs 3-1 4-point gold stars, all on khaki shoulder straps or looped slides. To avoid British troops mistaking Yugoslav junior NCOs (with their peaked caps and rank 'pips') for officers, from late 1941 the latter also wore 3-1 khaki or tropical white British sleeve chevrons points-down, changing from Mar 1942 to points-up chevrons.

Second-pattern rank insignia (8 Aug 1942–7 May 1945) On British khaki uniforms all ranks wore brass 6-point stars. General officers wore a Yugoslav or British crown above crossed swords above 3-1 stars; field officers, crown above 3-1 stars: subaltern officers, 4-1 stars; WOs, brass crown above 2-0 gold braid bars on both forearms; NCOs, crown above 3 chevrons points-up, and 3-1 chevrons points-up, on both upper sleeves.

7 (Yugoslavian) Troop, No.10 (Inter-Allied) Commando

10 (Inter-Allied) Commando was authorized on 29 June 1942, and by mid-1943 comprised 8 main numbered Troops, each with an establishment of 4 officers and 83 NCOs and men. The personnel were volunteers from Allied contingents in Britain or the Middle East, who were trained for intelligence and raiding operations in their occupied homelands. In August 1943 *Poručnik* Lochić and *Poručnik* Tripović, *Potporučnik* Tripović, and 16 'other ranks' formed 7 (Yugoslavian) Troop, under British Lt James Monahan, but it never exceeded 25 all ranks.

7 Troop transferred to Italy in Dec 1943 with 2 Special Service Bde, and in Feb 1944 deployed to the Adriatic island of Vis, already garrisoned by Tito's Partisans; there the Troop joined Force 144, supporting Partisan amphibious operations. Discipline suffered as personnel split into pro-Mihailović and pro-Tito camps, and on 15 Apr 1944 the Troop was disbanded.

Yugoslav Air Force

From Dec 1942, suitable refugee Yugoslav personnel were posted to RAF Aircraft Delivery Units, and then transferred individually to combat squadrons. In Sept 1943, B Flight of No. 94 Sqn South African Air Force in the Desert Air Force was manned by Yugoslavs flying Hurricanes, later Spitfires, but was disbanded 22 Aug 1944. The multi-national Balkan Air Force (7 June 1944–15 July 1945) was formed in Italy to support the Partisan forces in Yugoslavia. It comprised 4 RAF wings with 17 sqns, including Yugoslav Nos. 352 (Y) and 351 (Y) Sqns (formed 22 Apr and 1 July 1944 respectively); both initially flew Hurricanes, No. 352 later converting to Spitfires. Personnel wore RAF uniforms with Partisan rank tabs; officers also wore RAF rank insignia. The sqns disbanded on 15 June 1945, all personnel refusing repatriation.

1943: The deputy commander of the Royal Guards Bn, the Slovene officer *Potpukovnik* (LtCol) Josip Rijavec (left), photographed with one of his subalterns. Both wear British KD uniform and partial 37 Pattern webbing equipment, the subaltern with the greenish-grey Yugoslav M1939 *šajkaca*. Rijavec displays on both sleeves the formation patch of 10th Indian Inf Div: red-over-blue crossed diagonal bars on a black square. (Courtesy Nani Poljanec)

A navigator officer of the Yugoslav Detachment within the USAAF 15th Air Force's 512th Bombardment Squadron in Italy, 1944–45. On the US Army officers' 'chocolate' service cap (dark OD shade 51) he wears the M1937 Royal Yugoslav Air Force officers' silver-wire field-cap badge. On his 'chocolate' tunic he displays the silver Yugoslav M1937 observer's qualification badge on his right breast, and US navigator's silver 'wings' on his left. The Detachment's badge, painted on aircraft and sewn to flight jackets, was a black skull, crossbones and propeller, on a white disc edged red. (Courtesy Aleksandar Kolo)

On 25 Nov 1943 the Yugoslav Detachment (*Jugoslovenski odred*) formed from 40 Air Force personnel was attached to 512th Sqn, 376th Bomb Grp, US 15 Air Force in Italy, flying B-24 Liberator heavy bombers. Personnel wore US Army M1941 visored service caps with Yugoslav M1937 officers' or NCOs' capbadges; they held Yugoslav rank titles, but otherwise wore USAAF insignia. Of the Detachment's four Liberators, aircraft No. 23 survived the war, but the others were shot down (No. 22 over Sofia, Bulgaria, 24 Nov 1943; No. 21, Augsburg, Germany, 19 Dec 1943; and No. 20, Lobau, Austria, 22 Aug 1944). On 24 Aug 1945 the Detachment, reduced to 14 aircrew through casualties, transfers and defections to the Partisans, was disbanded, with 13 personnel transferring to the USAAF.

YUGOSLAV ARMY IN THE HOMELAND, 1941–45

1941: Formation of the Chetniks

In mid-April 1941 Col Dragoljub 'Draža' Mihailović and Army stragglers formed a guerilla force to fight the Axis. Mihailović headed for German-occupied Serbia, and on 13 May established his HQ on Mount Ravna Gora, near Valjevo. From mid-May to Aug Mihailović expanded his forces, named on 13 May 'Chetnik Detachments of the Yugoslav Army' (*Četnički odredi jugoslovenske vojske),* and later redesignated 'Military–Chetnik Detachments' (*Vojno–četnički odredi).* On 31 Aug 1941 Chetniks occupied Loznica on the Drina river in Western Serbia – the first town to be liberated in occupied Europe. This was followed by Bogatić (1 Sept, 1941), Krupanj (4 Sept), Banja Koviljača (6 Sept), Gornji Milanovac (29 Sept), Čačak (1 Oct), Stragari (4 Oct) and Ljubovija.

Meanwhile, on 7 July 1941, after Hitler's invasion of the Soviet Union, Tito's Partisans (see 'Yugoslav Liberation Army', below) proclaimed a general uprising, and in W Serbia established the 6,500-square mile 'Užice Republic' on 24 September. During that month, Mihailović organized 10,000 Chetniks into 27 company-sized Detachments (*odredi*) in four Commands (see also Table 3, page 31):

W Serbia: Avala, Cer, Crna Gora (Montenegro), Gledić, Gornji Milanovac, Gruža, Jadar, Kačer, Jelica, Kosmaj, Juhor, Kalaitović, Ljubić, Pozavina, Požega, Ribnica, Rudnik, Takovo, Užice, Valjevo, Žiča, Zlatibor.
E Serbia: Žagubica. **S Serbia**: Niš, Rasina, Vranje. **Bosnia**: Dangić.

Mihailović also commanded Serbs from Lika, SW Croatia, Montenegro and Slovenia. The isolated **Slovene Command** under Karlo Novak formed the 300–400 strong 'Blue Guard' (*Plava Garda*) in Apr 1941, and in May Mihailović renamed it the 'Royal Yugoslav Army in Slovenia' (*Kraljevska jugoslovenska vojska u Sloveniji*). It comprised three *odredi* (Carniola, Soča and Styria), expanded from 1942 into four nominal Corps. After the Slovenes' defeat by the Partisans at Grčarice (7–10 Sept 1943), Novak transferred command to Ivan Prezelje.

Chetniks and Partisans attacked German forces together in Aug 1941. Mihailović had opposed joint action, but eventually accepted that he must fight the Germans or lose credibility with the Allies. Chetniks and Partisans only fought in two joint actions: Šabac, Cer Det (22–24 Sept 1941), and the siege of Kraljevo

(continued on page 29)

YUGOSLAV ARMY, APRIL 1941
1: *Kapetan I kl.,* Infantry – Mech Bn
2: *Armijski djeneral*
3: *Kaplar,* Infantry

A

YUGOSLAV ARMY, APRIL 1941
1: *Podnarednik*, 3rd Bn, 1st Mtn Inf Regt
2: *Redov,* Guards Cavalry Bde
3: *Narednik vodnik III kl.,* AA Artillery

B

YUGOSLAV ARMY, APRIL 1941
1: *Poručnik*, 1st Tank Bn
2: *Narednik*, Chetnik Assault Bn
3: *Potporučnik,* 1st Parachute Co
3a: Air Force parachute badge

C

D

CHETNIKS, 1941–45
1: *Narednik* Perović; Bosnia, 1942
2: *Armijski djeneral* Mihailović; Serbia, August 1944
3: *Major* Raković; Serbia, 1944

E

CHETNIKS & PARTISANS, 1941–42
1: *Borac*, Partisan Detachments; Serbia, July 1941
2: *Vojvoda* Djujić, Chetniks; Croatia, 1942
3: *Komandant bataljona,* Partisan Dets; Croatia, March 1942

F

PARTISANS, 1943–44
1: *Vodnik;* Slovenia, December 1943
2: *Borac*, 2nd Proletarian Bde; March 1943
3: *General-lajtnant* Dapcević; Belgrade, Oct 1944

G

PARTISANS, 1944–45
1: *Potporučnik*, 1st Tank Bde; Šibenik, Oct 1944
2: *Maršal Jugoslavije* Tito, Oct 1944
3: *Stariji vodnik*, 4th Army; Trieste, May 1945

3

2

1

H

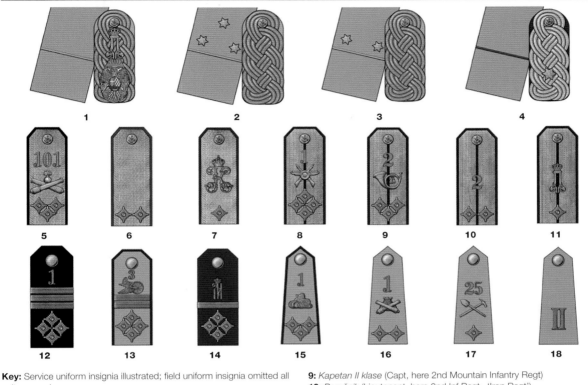

Key: Service uniform insignia illustrated; field uniform insignia omitted all unit numerals.

1: *Vojvoda* (Field-Marshal, here with King Peter II monogram)
2: *Armijski djeneral* (General)
3: *Divizijski djeneral* (MajGen)
4: *Brigadni djeneral* (Brigadier, here Cavalry; May–Dec 1939)
5: *Pukovnik* (Colonel, here 101st Motorized Artillery Bn)
6: *Djeneralštabni potpukovnik* (LtCol, here General Staff)
7: *Major* (Maj, here 4th Grand Duke Konstantin Konstantinović Cavalry Regt)
8: *Kapetan I klase* (Senior Captain, here 1st Mechanized Bn)

9: *Kapetan II klase* (Capt, here 2nd Mountain Infantry Regt)
10: *Poručnik* (Lieutenant, here 2nd Inf Regt –'Iron Regt')
11: *Potporučnik* (2nd Lt, here Royal Guard Inf Regt)
12: *Narednik-vodnik I klase* (Warrant Officer 1st Class, here 1st Assault Bn)
13: *Narednik-vodnik II klase* (WO 2nd Class, here 3rd Motorcycle Bn)
14: *Narednik-vodnik III klase* (WO 3rd Class, here 5th Queen Maria Cav Regt)
15: *Narednik* (Sergeant, here 1st Tank Bn)
16: *Podnarednik* (Corporal, here 1st Fortress Arty Regt)
17: *Kaplar* (Lance-Cpl, here 25th Divisional Engineer Regt)
18: *Redov* (Private, here 2nd Bicycle Bn, plus wheel badge on collar)

(9–31 October). Tito and Mihailović met at Struganik (19 Sept), Brajići (27 Oct), Čačak (18–20 Nov) and Pranjani, but failed to reach an understanding. By 31 Oct cooperation ceased, and henceforth Chetniks and Partisans were enemies, who fought each other mercilessly. Mihailović believed the Partisans posed a longer-term threat than the Germans. Crucially, he refused to expose Serbian civilians to the brutal German reprisal policy by provoking the occupiers. The Germans threatened to execute 50 Serbs for one wounded German,100 for one dead, and 1,000 for a senior officer killed. This was graphically illustrated by the Kragujevac massacre of 21 Oct 1941, when perhaps 2,794 Serb hostages were killed in reprisal for 10 Germans killed and 26 wounded, and in Kraljevo on 15 Oct, when 2,190 were executed.

In Sept 1941 Mihailović was recognized by the Yugoslav exile and British governments as leader of the Yugoslav resistance; in Dec he was promoted *brigadni djeneral*, on 19 Jan 1942 *divizijski djeneral*, and on 17 June *armijski djeneral*. From Sept 1941, Britain sent about 30 military missions to Yugoslavia under British liaison officers (BLOs) from Special

Autumn 1941: Chetniks wearing a mixture of uniforms and civilian dress escort German prisoners-of-war through a town in Western Serbia. From 1945, Tito's Communist propaganda machine only showed images of Germans captured by Partisans. (Military Museum, Belgrade)

Operations Executive (SOE). Three missions – under Maj 'Bill' Hudson (25 Oct 1941–Mar 1944), Col William Bailey (25 Dec 1942–Feb 1944), and Brig Charles Armstrong (Oct 1943–May 1944) – were accredited to Mihailović, but he complained that supplies airlifted in between 9 Nov 1941 and 10 Dec 1943 were inadequate.

On 1 Nov 1941, Chetnik forces attacked Požega and Partisan HQ at Užice, but the Partisans forced them back to Ravna Gora. Mihailović was now desperate, and on 11 Nov Chetnik officers met German commanders at Divci; both sides rejected cooperation, although 3,551 Chetniks joined Gen Nedić's tolerated Serbian forces as 'Legalized Chetniks'.

On 15 Nov the Partisans besieged Ravna Gora, but on 21 Nov Gen Nedić sent reinforcements, and the Chetniks captured Užice. On 6–7 Dec the Germans took Ravna Gora in Op 'Mihailović', but the Chetniks escaped to Sandžak. Meanwhile, on 29 Nov German forces occupied Užice in Op 'Užice' (in Partisan terms, the '1st Enemy Offensive'), but Tito escaped into Bosnia.

1942: Establishment

On 11 Jan 1942 the Yugoslav exile government appointed Mihailović Minister of Defence of the 'Yugoslav Army in the Homeland' (*Jugoslovenska vojska u otadžbini* – JvuO), and on 10 June he was appointed Chief of Staff of its Supreme Command. In early 1942 the JVuO's organization was revised.

The basic unit was the brigade *(brigada)* with 2–5 battalions, a bn *(bataljon)* having 2–4 companies. A company *(četa)* was organized as either Category 3 (mobile troops, aged 20–31); Cat 2 (sabotage troops, aged 31–40), or Cat 1 (village guards, aged 41–50). A company was divided into platoons, a ptn *(vod)* having 3 sections (sing: *odeljenje*). In practice these designations were greatly inflated, and a 4-bn 'bde' mustered only about 400 fighters. Women served as clerks and nurses. In spring 1942 the JvuO Supreme Command moved from W Serbia to Bosna–Herzegovina, and in June to Italian-occupied Montenegro.

Most Chetnik units were static, kept in their home districts to protect local Serbs. Commanders minimized cooperation with their neighbours, and avoided casualties, while hoping for an Allied landing in Dalmatia. From summer 1942 to Mar 1943 the Germans reorganized the 'Legalized Chetnik' detachments into auxiliaries to serve with the Italian, Croatian, or Gen Nedić's Serbian troops.

In June 1942 the Soviet Union switched support from the Chetniks to the Partisans, condemning Mihailović as a simple collaborator – a misrepresentation, which was based on temporary local agreements which Chetnik commanders certainly concluded with Axis forces, while remaining basically loyal to the London government.

The BLOs encouraged Mihailović to become more aggressive. Some 8,000 Partisans failed to capture Chetnik-held Bosansko Grahovo, W Bosnia, on 21–29 June. Between 30 July and Oct 1942, Chetniks derailed

10 Axis trains, sabotaging track and railway buildings and destroying the Počekovina and Stopanja bridges. This earned a commendation in Dec from Gen Alexander for supporting the Allied build-up for El Alamein, but 27,000 Serb hostages were executed by the Germans.

In Nov 1942 the Chetniks established a Youth wing, the 'Yugoslav Ravna Gora Youth' (*Jugoslovenska ravnogorska omladina* – JURAO), with special university, high school and other branches. JURAO members were liable for call-up to Chetnik forces.

1943: Civil war

On 1 Jan 1943 the Chetniks were again reorganized. The higher formation became the corps (*korpus*) with 500–2,000 men in 3–5 bdes, each bde nominally comprising 3 battalions. The bn had 3 companies (including labour cos); the co had 45–90 men in three ptns, each ptn (*vod*) containing 5–15 *trojkas* of 3 men – a traditional Serbian practice. An élite mobile bde, operating across corps district boundaries, was designated a 'flying brigade' (*leteća brigada*). A few bdes were joined

A young Chetnik of Gen Mihailović's bodyguard unit, with British uniform and a Mk 2 Sten gun, apart from the *šajkača* with an M1939 NCOs' capbadge. The locally-made silver 'Ravna Gora' badge above his left breast pocket comprises a crowned double-headed eagle with a Serbian shield, and the Chetnik motto *'Sloboda ili smrt'* ('Freedom or Death'). It commemorates the mountain where the Chetnik guerrilla movement was founded on 13 May 1941. (Miloslav Samardzić 'Pogledi' Archive)

A machine-gun unit of the 3rd Žica 'Flying' Brigade of the 2nd Ravnogorski Corps, armed with captured German MG 34s. The Chetniks wear Yugoslav Army uniforms; in this case they too have grown their hair long, but do not wear beards. (Miloslav Samardzić 'Pogledi' Archive)

together as 'groups of brigades' (sing: *grupa brigade*). Total active strength in late 1943 was about 30,000, but 472,900 men (mostly Serbs) aged 18–40 were theoretically available for call-up, leaving 169,000 aged 40–55 for guard duties.

From Jan 1943, Mihailović both carried out sabotage missions and attacked Partisan units, although London ordered him to concentrate on German and Nedić's forces. During the '4th Enemy Offensive' against the Partisans, 12,000–15,000 Chetniks from Montenegro, E Bosnia and Herzegovina, with Italian support, failed to defend the Neretva river, allowing the Partisans to cross into E Herzegovina 20 Feb–15 Mar 1943. This was the high point in Chetnik–Axis cooperation, and the beginning of Mihailović's decline. The battle of the Sutjeska ('5th Enemy Offensive', 15 May–16 June) followed, with Axis forces driving the Partisans into E Bosnia; they then disarmed 7,000 Chetniks in Montenegro, Sandžak and Herzegovina, driving Mihailović from Montenegro into Serbia.

Most Partisans and Chetniks in Croatia and Dalmatia were ethnic Serbs who joined in response to *Ustasha* atrocities, but following the surrender of Italy to the Allies on 8 Sept 1943 Croats began to join the Partisans in increasing numbers; this deprived the Chetniks of supplies, while the growing Partisan forces took over Lika, much of N Dalmatia, W Bosnia, Herzegovina and Montenegro. Meanwhile the Chetniks in Serbia continued sabotage missions, destroying the Mokra Gora railway bridge near Užice in Oct 1943, and on 6 Oct capturing Višegrad and destroying the Drina Bridge over the Sarajevo–Užice railway (the largest railway bridge sabotaged in occupied Europe). However, despite protests from the BLOs attached with Mihailović, BBC London persistently credited the Partisans with these successes.

In Oct 1943 Mihailović moved from Serbia to E Bosnia, but Chetniks and Italian auxiliaries had little success against either Germans or Partisans in Bosnia, Dalmatia and Montenegro during Sept–Dec 1943. A Chetnik attack on Sarajevo was foiled by the Partisans, who occupied Goražde and Foča. Meanwhile, the Chetnik Dinara Div attacked Dubrovnik, halting the Partisan advance. Chetniks liberated Prijepolje and Priboj (12 Sept 1943); Zvornik and Banja Koviljača (17 Sept); Bijelo Polje (Sept); Rudo and Brza

Palanka (18 Sept); Ljubovija and Bajina Bašta (30 Sept); Nova Varoš (Oct); Višegrad (5 Oct); Čajetina (10 Oct), and Rogatica (14 October).

Between 13 Nov 1943 and 31 Mar 1944 Chetnik officers concluded four short-term renewable cooperation agreements with German forces – a controversial strategy which split Chetnik opinion. Meanwhile the Rasina–Toplica Group of Corps from Sandžak supported the unsuccessful German Op 'Kugelblitz' (2–18 Dec 1943) to prevent E Bosnian Partisans from entering Serbia.

At the Teheran Conference (28 Nov–1 Dec), Roosevelt, Churchill and Stalin agreed to abandon Mihailović in favour of Tito, thus ensuring the eventual defeat of the Chetniks.

1944: The defence of Serbia

In early Mar 1944 the British withdrew recognition and aid from the Chetniks. In May, Mihailović was dismissed as Minister of Defence and in Aug he lost the Supreme Command, but he retained field command.

By 1944 the Chetniks numbered about 30,000 men in 11 Commands, with Coastal District retaining the traditional title 'Division' (Divizija). 87 'corps' were formed, and from Nov 'groups of corps' (sing: grupa korpusa – GK) were assembled, each with 2–3 corps. The Supreme Command included six élite 'shock corps' (sing: jurišni korpus – JK). The largest formation was IV Group of Shock Corps (IV Grupa jurišnih korpusa – IV GJK) formed June 1944 under Major Dragoslav Račić, with 8,000–9,000 men.

The Montenegrin Volunteer Corps (Crnogorski dobrovoljački korpus – CDK) was formed Jan 1944 as a Chetnik unit under Vojvoda Pavle Djurišić, and organized Apr 1944 into 7 named bns (Bjelopavlići, Čevo, Crmničani, Komani, Lješnjani, Riječani, Vasojevići–Kuči).

The US Office of Strategic Services (OSS) had sent Mihailović three liaison officers between Aug–Sept 1943 and Feb–Mar 1944, and Capt Mansfield, LtCol Seitz and Lt Musulin reported no Chetnik–Axis collaboration. Later, under the OSS's Op 'Halyard' (a.k.a. 'Air Bridge'), based in Pranjani near Gornji Milanovac in W Serbia, Capt Musulin's 1st Aircrew Rescue Unit rescued 537 downed Allied airmen (345 Americans, 192 others) between 9 Aug and 27 Dec 1944. Those rescued were evacuated by air from Pranjani to Bari; the largest such US operation in World War II, this would remain classified by the State Dept until 1968.

The Germans undertook four operations against Partisans invading Serbia. In Op 'Kammerjäger' in mid-Mar they halted them after eight weeks' heavy fighting, with the Chetniks contributing 10,000 men in six corps (Javor, II Kosovo, Požega, Rasina, I & II Ravna Gora). In Op 'Trumpf' (10–19 July) Axis forces, including Chetnik IV GJK and Rasina–Kopaonik GK, failed to eliminate Partisans advancing from the south into Central Serbia; and in Op 'Draufgänger' (18 July–1 Aug) they could not prevent Partisans advancing from Montenegro into Serbia. In Op 'Rübezahl' (12–30 Aug) Axis forces, including the Montenegrin 1st & 3rd Regts CDK, decisively defeated Partisans on Mount Durmitor, but the Partisans escaped to SW Serbia.

On 17 Aug many Chetniks accepted an amnesty from the Partisans. On 1 Sept, Mihailović announced a general Chetnik mobilization in Serbia, producing 30,000–40,000 men. Chetniks liberated Majdanpek (26 Aug); Kučevo (28 Aug); Leskovac and Vlasotince (31 Aug); Svrljig (2 Sept) and Lazarevac (3 Sept); Pljevlja (Sept), Varvarin (Oct) and Kruševac (14 October).

Aaron Rengel (alias Yan Strichitz) was one of a number of Jewish guerrillas who joined Chetnik units in Eastern Serbia to escape slave labour in the infamous Bor copper mines (notable among them was Dr Tibor Goldwan, chief of the Medical Dept of the Chetnik Supreme Command). Rengel is wearing an M1939 *šajkača* with the NCOs' capbadge, and a locally-made version of the British battledress blouse above Yugoslav breeches, puttees, and mountain socks and boots. See under Plate G1 for details of the Yugoslav hand grenades hanging from his belt. (Miloslav Samardzić 'Pogledi' Archive)

A hirsute *kapetan II klase* of the Chetniks, photographed in Belanovica, Central Serbia; his rank under the April 1944 regulations is shown by three diagonal yellow bars on his left forearm. High on the same sleeve he wears an unidentified home-made unit patch. His brass capbadge is that of the old Chetnik Association: a skull-and-crossbones and crossed bayonets, on a double-headed Serbian eagle. Note the light anti-tank gun in the background. (Miloslav Samardzić 'Pogledi' Archive)

Tito had continued his build-up in Serbia, and by Oct counted 16 divisions. On 5 Sept, IV GJK attacked Partisans from Sandžak, but were defeated 9 Sept at Jelova Gora near Uziče; nearly captured, Mihailović escaped to NE Bosnia. On 12 Sept King Petar, under British pressure, broadcast to all Yugoslavs to join Tito and reject Mihailović, which further damaged morale.

On 6 Oct 1944, Gen Nedić's Serbian State Guard (SDS) and Frontier Guard (SGS) re-formed into the Chetnik Serbian Assault Corps (Srpski Udarni Korpus – SUK) with 8 bdes in 3 divs: 1 SUK Div (ex-SDS) – 1–3 bdes; 2 SUK Div (ex-SDS) – 4–6 bdes; 3 SUK Div (ex-SGS) – 7–8 brigades. The SUK's failure to recapture Tuzla, E Bosnia in Dec 1944 would lead to its disbandment in Jan 1945.

Chetnik defeats forced a general retreat to NW Serbia. On 2 Oct, IV GJK retreated to Central Serbia. Soviet and Partisan forces occupied Belgrade 11–20 Oct, and Chetnik attempts at cooperation were vetoed by Stalin. By 20 Oct Chetnik forces were retreating to Sandžak and then NE Bosnia. The loss of Serbia, the Partisans' military successes, and British and Soviet hostility fatally compromised Chetnik prospects, forcing them to keep on good terms with the Germans.

1945: Defeat

Mihailović still hoped for an Allied landing, or an anti-Communist rising in Serbia. In Jan 1945 he even planned a new federal army, with Serbian, Croatian and Slovene Armies and a Moslem Group of Corps. Another possibility was to join with 35,000 Chetnik and Yugoslav collaborationist forces in the Ljubljana Gap, and surrender to the British 8 Army which had fought its way up Italy.

In mid-Jan Mihailović and his troops moved to Mount Trebava, NE Bosnia, linking with Djurišić's 7,000-strong Montenegrin Volunteer Corps (CDK), organized into 3 regts (1–3), each with 2 battalions. In March, Mihailović moved to Mount Vučjak, NW Bosnia. He wanted to return to Serbia, while Djurišić aimed for the Ljubljana Gap. On 18 Mar the CDK set off for Ljubljana, but was heavily defeated at Lijevče Polje, N Bosnia by Croatian forces. Mihailović sent Gen Damjanović to the Ljubljana Gap to rally Chetnik troops, but the Chetniks moved on 5 May to Palmanova, NE Italy, and surrendered to the British. Meanwhile, on 13 Apr Mihailović and 12,000 Chetniks had left Vučjak for Serbia, braving Croatian and Partisan ambushes, but suffering final defeat by the Partisans on 13 May at Zelengora, Bosnia.

Mihailović was captured by Partisans on 13 Mar 1946 near Višegrad, E Bosnia; he was tried, and shot by firing squad in Belgrade on 17 July 1948. He was always a Serbian patriot, but he lacked the necessary military skills, or a political programme, for the impossible task of uniting the Yugoslav nations.

Uniforms & insignia

From May 1941 Chetniks wore pre-1941 Yugoslav Army or Air Force uniforms, eventually replaced with Axis, British or civilian items, although often retaining the M1939 *šajkača* or M1940 Chetnik Assault Troops' black *kalpak* with M1939 officers' or NCOs' capbadges.

Rank titles were retained (the highest being *armijski djeneral)* and personnel received regular promotions, but shoulder-strap rank insignia were usually omitted. On 7 Apr 1944 rank insignia were introduced, comprising narrow (1cm) and medium (1.5cm) yellow or white braid diagonal bars 6cm long, worn on a cloth patch of any colour on the left forearm only. Field officers wore 3-1 narrow above 1 medium yellow bars; subaltern officers, 4-1 narrow yellow bars; *narednik-vodnik.* 4 narrow white bars; NCOs, 3-1 narrow white bars.

YUGOSLAV PEOPLE'S LIBERATION ARMY, 1941–45

1941: Organization

The most successful guerrilla commander of World War II was the General Secretary of the Communist Party of Yugoslavia (KPJ), Jŏsip 'Tito' Brôz. On 10 Apr 1941, as Yugoslavia collapsed in defeat, Tito formed a military committee; however, Stalin vetoed military action, as Germany was still technically a Soviet ally under the Aug 1939 Molotov–Ribbentrop non-aggression pact. Following Germany's invasion of the USSR on 22 June 1941, on 27 June Tito was appointed commander-in-chief of guerrilla forces of all political parties and ethnic groups in the United National Liberation Front (UNOF).

On 27 June the National Liberation Partisan Detachments of Yugoslavia *(Narodnooslobodilački partizanski odredi Jugoslavije* – NOPOJ) were formed, commanded by an HQ *(Glavni štab* – GŠ), later redesignated GHQ *(Vrhovni štab* – VŠ). Six Partisan Districts, each with HQs, were formed in 1941, controlling 61 Detachments.

The Croatian GŠ was formed on 19 Aug 1941, controlling the National Liberation Movement in Croatia *(Narodnooslobodački pokret u Hrvatskoj* – NOP), which aimed to free Croatia from both Axis occupation and the *Ustasha* dictatorship. By Dec 1941 the NOP was the most effective Partisan force outside Serbia, with 7,000 personnel, including 5,400 local Serbs; by late 1944 it would number 150,000, mostly Croats. The other Districts were Serbia (formed 4 July 1941), Montenegro and Boka Kotor (Oct 1941); Sandžak (Oct 1941); Bosnia–Herzegovina (13 July 1941) and Pokrajina/ Vardar Macedonia (Nov 1941). The Yugoslav Communist Party controlled all Partisans except in Slovenia. There the Liberation Front *(Osvobodilna fronta* – OF), formed 27 Apr, represented a wide political coalition with the Slovene Partisans as its military arm.

The standard military unit was the Detachment *(Odred)*, named after a town or geographical feature. A detachment was controlled by a regional HQ *(Glavni štab)*, and divided into 2–3 companies of 80–100 men; larger detachments had 2–4 battalions. Companies had 2–3 ptns (sing: *vod)*, divided into sections (sing: *desetina)*.

Uprisings

The Partisan uprisings were formally declared in Belgrade (4 July 1941), Montenegro (13 July), Slovenia (22 July), Croatia and Bosnia–Herzegovina (27 July), and Macedonia (11 October). In 1941–42 Serbs were the dominant nationality in Partisan units except in Slovenia. The 1st Split

Partisans were defeated at Split, Dalmatia (26 Aug), and the Kapaonik Det defended the 'Miners' Republic', Stanulovice, Serbia (10 Aug–11 September). From 28 July to 1 Dec 1941 Tito sustained a Partisan enclave, the 'Užice Republic', in W Serbia, but was defeated in the German '1st Enemy Offensive', escaping on 29 Nov to E Bosnia – where he received a cold reception from Serbs who overwhelmingly favoured Mihailovič.

1942: Organization
(see also Table 4, page 38)

In Jan 1942 the Partisans were redesignated the National Liberation Partisan and Volunteer Army of Yugoslavia (*Narodnooslobodilačka partizanska i dobrovoljačka vojska Jugoslavije* – NOP i DVJ). Subsequently 3 more District HQs were formed: Vojvodina and Banat (1942); Kosovo–Metohija, and Syrmia (both Oct 1942). Pokrajina district was renamed 'Macedonia', but Slovenia remained independent of Tito until 1944, when it became the tenth HQ.

In 1942 Croatian HQ was reorganized into five Operational Zones (OZ, sing: *operativna zona*), but by early 1944 these had been redesignated Corps or Divs: 1 OZ (Jan–Nov 1942); 2 OZ (Mar–Jan 1944); 3 OZ (May 1942–June 1943); 4 OZ (11 July 1942–13 Feb 1943); 5 OZ (May–June 1943).

In Bosnia–Herzegovina, Tito formed in Jan 1942 the National Liberation Volunteer Army of Yugoslavia (*Narodnooslobodilačka dobrovoljačka vojska Jugoslavije*) in E Bosnia. There some 7,000 men in 7 Detachments were eager to fight with the Partisans, but rejected Tito's Communist ideology (and red star capbadge). This force was of dubious loyalty and military value, and disbanded in May 1942.

Brigades

The Brigade superseded (but did not replace) the Detachment as the key tactical unit. Brigade organization showed wide variations, but typically contained a Bde HQ with commander and commissar; mounted, eng, sigs and med ptns; plus 4 x 300-strong inf bns, each with 3–4 cos; heavy co with 2 MG and 2 mortar ptns; field arty, MT, and 'cultural-political' (Communist propaganda) units.

The title 'Shock', meaning 'Assault' (*Udarna* – U), was awarded to distinguished units, and 'Proletarian' (*Proleterski*) to the best of these shock units. The first Croatian Proletarian Bn was formed 7 May 1942 from three Proletarian Cos transferred from the Kordun, Coastal-Mtn and Lika Dets, and reported to GŠ NOP; on 10 Nov 1942 it joined 13. Proletarian Brigade. On 21 Dec 1942 the 1st Prol Shock Bde (*1. Proleterska udarna brigada*) was formed at Rudo, E Bosnia. It comprised 1,199 men in 6 shock bns each about 200 strong, representing different parts of Yugoslavia; this bde had 'shock bns' and 'shock

A group of senior Partisan commanders in Bosnia, autumn 1942: all wear locally-made uniforms with red star capbadges. (Left) Arso Jovanović, a Montenegrin General Staff *Kapetan I klase* appointed on 12 Dec 1941 as Chief of Staff of Partisan Supreme Command, and on 1 March 1945 as Yugoslav Army Chief of Staff. (2nd left) Josip Broz 'Tito', Partisan Supreme Commander, with his German Shepherd dog Luks, who on 9 June 1943 reportedly saved his life from a German bomb. (3rd left) Aleksandar Ranković, a Communist Party Secretary attached to the Supreme Command. The right-hand man is unidentified. (Courtesy Bojan Dimitrijević)

cos', better trained men and superior weaponry. (Again, as in the Chetniks, all units were actually smaller than their nominal titles suggest.)

In all, 213 bdes, including 20 Proletarian, were formed between 12 Dec 1941 and 7 Mar 1945, but did not all exist simultaneously. Most bdes were named after their military district, but many Croatian and Slovene bdes commemorated significant individuals.

Serbia: 1.–3. Serbian Proletarian Shock; 3., 9., 11.–20., 22.–29., 31. & 32. Serbia; 1.–7. S Morava; 1. & 2. Šumadija.

Croatia: 13. Croatia Prol; 1.–2. Dalmatia Prol Shock; 1.–3. Lika Prol Shock; 12. Slavonia Prol Shock; 13. Rade Končar/Josip Kraš Prol Shock; 4., 7., 8., 16. Banja; Brod; 3., 4., 6., 14. Coastal-Mtn; 3.–14. Dalmatia; Nikola Demonija; Matija Gobec; 1.–3. Istria; Jan Žiška Czechoslovak; Karlovac; 4., 5. Kordun; Paulek Mihovil Miškina; 1. &2. Moslavac; 1.–3. Moslem; Franjo Ogulinac-Seljo; Osijek; Brača Radić; 17., 18., 21. Slavonia; Virovitica; 4. Bde/7. Div; 3. Bde/8. Div; 3. Bde/13. Div; 1. Bde/33. Div; 1. Bde/35. Div; 16. Youth; Zagorje; Žumberak.

Montenegro & Boka Kotor: 4. & 5. Montenegro Prol Shock; 1. Boka Kotor; 5., 6.–10. Montenegro.

Sandžak: 3.Sandžak Prol Shock; 4. Sandžak.

Bosnia–Herzegovina: 6. E Bosnia Prol Shock; 1.–3. Krajina Prol Shock;14., 18. & 19. Central Bosnia; 18. & 21. E Bosnia; 10. Herzegovina Prol Shock; 11.–14. Herzegovina; 1., 2., 4.–13., 15.–17., 20. Krajina; 16. Moslem; 17. Majevica; 19. Birčana.

Pokrajina/Macedonia: 1. Macedonia–Kosovo Prol Shock; 1.–21. Macedonia; 4. Macedonia–Albania.

Vojvodina & Banat: 1.–15. Vojvodina.

Kosovo–Metohija: 1.–8. Kosovo–Metohija.

Slovenia: 1. Prole Shock Tome Tomšic'; 2. Matija Gubec; 3. Ivan Cankar; 4. Ljubo Šercer; 5. Simon Gregorčič; 6. Ivan Gradnik; 6. Slavko Šlander; 7. Francè Prešern; 8. Fran Levistik; 9. Slovenia; 10. Ljubljana; 11. Miloš Zidanšek; 12. Slovenia; 13. Mirko Bračič; 14. Snežnik; 14. Trst; 14. Železničarska; 15. Bela Krajina; 16. Simon Gegorčič; 16. Janko Premrl-Vojkp; 17. Simon Gegorčič; 19. Srechko Kosovel; 20. Goriška; 20. Štabna; 24. Fontanok; 2. & 3. Soča; Idrijska; Rab.

Detachments

The traditional Yugoslav guerrilla unit, the Detachment, remained popular in spite of successive reorganizations, but it was still temporary, used for small-scale tasks such as guard duty. Sizes varied from co (50 men) to bn (150). In all, 239 Detachments were formed between June 1941 and May 1945, each named after a village or geographical feature. In Serbia there were 45; Bosnia–Herzegovina, 53; Montenegro–Sandžak,15; Croatia, 76; Macedonia–Slovenia, 26; and in Vojvodina, 3.

Campaigns

The '2nd Enemy Offensive' comprised three local German–Croat operations. In Op 'South-East Croatia' (15–23 Jan 1942), Germans and Croats attempted to encircle Birač, Majevica, Ozren, Romanjia, Zvijezda and Kalinovik Partisan Dets in the Tuzla–Višegrad–Sarajevo region of E Bosnia. The Romanija Det, supported by 1st Prol Shock Bde, held the line in freezing snow, suffering significant casualties. In Op 'Ozren' (26 Jan–4 Feb), Axis forces planned to trap 2,000 Partisans between the

The clothing of this Serbian guerrilla photographed in mid-1941 might suggest either a Chetnik or a Partisan, but the latter is more likely, since he displays no capbadge. In the first four months of the war Moscow instructed the Partisans to expand their appeal among non- Communists, so they did not adopt the red star badge until October 1941. This fighter wears the familiar Yugoslav Army M1939 *šajkača* and a tunic without shoulder straps, combined with peasants' black *pantalone* breeches, *charape* knee-length socks, and brown *opanci* shoes. (Dušan Babac Collection)

Table 4: Yugoslav People's Liberation Army order of battle, 11 January 1943–8 May 1945

1. Army (1.1.1945): 1 Prol Corps : 1, 5, 6,11, 21 Divs; 15 Corps (3.4.1945): 42, 48 Divs); 2, 17, 22 Divs; 2 Tank Bde.

2. Army (1.1.1945 < South Operational Group of Divs): 14 Corps (23, 25, 45 Divs); 1 Army Group (17, 28 Divs). Sarajevo Task Force (2, 3, 5 Corps).

3. Army (1.1.1945): GS Vojvodina; 12 Corps (16, 36, 51 Divs); 12 Slavoniia Corps (17, 32, 33, 40 Divs).

4. Army (1.3.1945): 7 Corps (14, 18 Divs); 8 Corps (9, 19, 20, 26 Divs); 11 Corps (13, 35, 43 Divs); 9 Corps (30, 31 Divs); 1 Tank Bde (17 Jul 1944) (1-4 Tank, Eng Bns); Art, Eng, Replacement Bdes; Mot Arty Bn; Sigs Regt.

1 Bosnia Corps (9.11.1942 > 3 Corps (5.10.1943): 4, 5 Div; **1 Croatia Corps** (22.11.1942) > 4 Corps (7.10.1943): 6–8 Divs; **2 Bosnia Corps** (22.11.1942) > 5 Corps (1.5.1943): 4, 10 Divs. **1 Slavonia Corps** (17.5.1943) > 2 Croatian Corps (20.6.1943) > 6 Corps (7.10.1943): 4, 12, 20, 28 Divs. **2 Shock Corps** (10.9.1943): 2 Prol, 3 Shock, 20 Divs; **7 Corps** (3.10.1943):- 14, 15, 18 Divs. **1 Proletarian Corps** (5.10.1943): 1, 6 Prol Divs. **8 Corps** (7.10.1943): 9, 19, 20, 26 Divs. **9 Corps** (19.12.1943): 32, 33 Divs; **10 Corps** (22.12.1943): 30, 31 Divs. **11 Corps** (30.1.1944): 13, 35 Divs (6.9.1944). **12 Corps** (1.7.1944): 16, 36 Divs. **13 Corps** (7.9 /7.12.1944): 22, 24 Divs. **14 Corps** (6.9.1944): 23, 25, 45 Divs. **15 Corps** (9.1944): 41, 46, 49 Divs. **16 Corps** (9 / 6.12.1944): 42, Kumanovo Divs. **Bregalnica–Strumica Corps** (3.10.–6.12.1944): 50, 51 Divs.

1 Proletarian Shock Div (1.11.1942); **2 Proletarian Shock Div** (1.11.1942); **3 Montenegro NO Shock Div** (9.11.1942); **4 Krajina NO Shock Div** (9.11.1942) > 12 Krajina NO Div (9.5.1943) > 12 Krajina NO Shock Div (11.10.1944) **5 Krajina NO Shock Div** (9.11.1942); **6 NO Lika Div** (22.11.1942) >'Nikola Tesla' Proletarian Div (19.3.1944); **7 Banija NO Div** (22.11.1942) > 7 Banija NO Shock Div (9.1943); **8 Kordun NO Div** (22.11.1942) > 8 Kordun NO Shock Div (3.12.1944); **9 Dalmatia NO Div** (13.2/12.4.1943) > 9 Dalmatia NO Shock Div (3.12.1944); **10 Bosnia NO Shock Div** (1.4.1943); 4 Croatia Div (9.5.1943) >**12 Slavonia NO Div** (30.12.1942) > 12 Shock Div (11.1944); **12 Krajina NO Div** (1.6.1943) > 11 Krajina NO Shock Div (19.8.1943); **13 Coastal–Mountain NO Div** (4.1943) > 13 Coastal–Mountain NO Shock Div (21.12.1944); **14 Slovenia NO Div** (13.7.1943) > 14 Slovenia NO Shock Div (26.10.1944); **15 Slovenia NO Div** (13.7.1943); **16 Vojvodina NO Shock Div** (11.7.1943); **17 E Bosnia NO Shock Div** (2.7.1943); **18 Slovenia NO Div** (14.9.1943); **19 N Dalmatia NO Div** (10.1943) > 19 N Dalmatia NO Shock Div (10.11.1944); **20 Central Dalmatia NO Div** (20.5.1944) > 20 Central Dalmatia NO Shock Div (23.12.1944); 1 Serbia NO Div (20.5.1944) > **21 Serbia** NO Shock Div (20.5.1944) > 21 Serbia NO Shock Div (6.1944); 2 Serbia NO Div (22.5.1944) > **22 Serbia NO Div** (6.1944) > 22 Serbia NO Shock Div (6.1944); 3 Serbia NO Div (6.6.1944)> **23 Serbia NO Div** (6.1944); 4 Serbia NO Div (10.6.1944) > 24 **Serbia NO Div** (10.6.1944); **25 Serbia NO Div** (21.6.1944); **26 S Dalmatia NO Div** (10.1943) > 26 S Dalmatia NO Shock Div (`10.1944); 3 E Bosnia NO Div, 3 Corps (10.10.1943) > **27 E Bosnia NO Shock Div** (10.10.1943); 10 Croatian NO Shock (17.5.1943) > **28 Slavonia NO Div** (17.5.1943) > 28 Slavonia NO Shock Div (30.11.1943); Herzegovina NO Shock Div (21.12.1943) > 29 NO Shock Div (6.10.1943); Gorizia Div > 27 NO Div (12.1943) >32 NO Div (12.1943) > **30 Slovenia NO Div** (11.1944); Triglav Div (6.10.1943) > 28 NO Div > **31 Slovenia NO Div** (12.1943); **32 Zagorska–Croatian NO Div** (12.12.1943) > **33 Croatian NO Div** (19.1.1944); **34 Croatian NO Div** (30.1.1944) > 34 Croatian NO Shock Div (1.1945); **35 Lika NO Div** (30.1.1944) > 35 Lika NO Shock Div (21.12.1944); **36 Vojvodina NO Shock Div** (3.3.1944); **37 Sandžak NO Shock Div** (4.3.1944); **38 Bosnia NO Shock Div** (6.3.1944); **39 Bosnia NO Div** (26.3.1944); **40 Slavonia NO Div** (15.7.1944) > 40 Slavonia NO Shock Div (5.2.1945); **41 Macedonia NO Div** (25.8.1944); **42 Macedonia NO Div** (7.9.1944)> 42 Macedonia NO Shock Div (12.1944); **43 Istria NO Div** (29.8.1944); **45 Serbia NO Div** (3.9.1944); **46 Serbia NO Div** (20.9.1944); **47 Serbia NO Div** (1.10.1944/5.1945); **48 Macedonia NO Div** (22.9.1944) > 48 Macedonia NO Shock Div (12.1944) ; **49 Macedonia NO Div** (10.9.1944); **50 Macedonia NO Div** (17.9./6.12.1944); 3 Vojvodina NO Shock Div (31.10.1943) > **51 Macedonia Div** (13.11.1944); > 50 Macedonia Div (6.12.1944); **Kumanovo Div** (10.1944); 3 Vojvodina NO Shock Div (31.10.1944) > 51 Vojvodina NO Shock Div (13.11.1944);; **52 Kosmet NO Div** (8.2.1945); Central Bosnia NO Shock Div (7.1944) > **53 Central Bosnia NO Shock Div** (12.1944).

rivers Bosna and Speča in E Bosnia, but the Partisans escaped to the Igman plateau, Sarajevo. In Op 'Prijedor' (mid-late Feb), NW Bosnia, German forces relieved that town's Croatian garrison, besieged by Partisans.

The three-stage '3rd Enemy Offensive' (Op 'Trio') was a German–Italian–Croat–Chetnik operation to trap and destroy 18,000 Partisans, including the élite 1st and 2nd Prol Bdes (8 Apr–14 June 1942). 'Trio I' (8–20 Apr), the relief of Rogatica's Croat garrison, was abandoned when the Croats attacked the Chetniks and the Partisans escaped. In 'Trio II' (20–30 Apr), Rogatica was relieved without a battle and Croat forces occupied the Drina river bend. In 'Trio III' (30 Apr–14 June), the Partisans retreated to Birač, E Bosnia, and in mid-May Chetniks and Italians occupied Partisan areas in Montenegro and Herzegovina.

In Jan–Mar 1942 the Partisans established the 'Foča Republic' in liberated territory around Foča and Goražde, E Bosnia. In spring they created a liberated territory between the Sava river and Mt Kozara, W Bosnia. This area suffered sustained German and Croat attacks in Op 'Kozara' (or 'West Bosnia') from 10 June until they ceased in Aug, having inflicted heavy casualties. The Partisans nevertheless managed to regain part of the free territory in September. By Dec

1942 the Partisans were a formidable military force, 236,000 strong, and able to attack and defeat German main-force troops.

1943: Organization
In Nov 1942 the NOP i DVJ was redesignated the National Liberation Army and Partisan Detachments of Yugoslavia *(Narodnooslobodilačka vojska i partizanski odredi Jugoslavije* – NOV i POJ), although it was popularly known simply as the People's Liberation Army *(Narodnooslobodilačka vojska* – NOV).

Divisions
On 1 Nov 1942 the 1st Proletarian Shock Bde was redesignated the 1st Proletarian Shock Division *(1. Proleterska udarna divizija)*. Thus the div had replaced the

Two Partisans wearing locally-made uniforms (cf Plate F3 for the 'three-peak' *triglavka* cap), manning an 8mm Schwarzlose MG in a position outside Jajce, Central Bosnia, 29–30 November 1943, while protecting the Second Session of the Anti-Fascist Council for the National Liberation of Yugoslavia (AVNOJ). This conference appointed Tito to marshal's rank and the position of national prime minister; refused to recognize the Yugoslav government-in-exile; and banned King Petar II Karadjordjević's return to Yugoslavia before a referendum to decide the future of the monarchy. (Museum of Yugoslavia, Belgrade)

bde as the main tactical formation, even though 'division' strength was only 2,000–4,000 men. A div comprised a Div HQ plus 3–4 bdes, usually from the same district; sometimes a bn-sized arty bde; and 1–4 Partisan detachments. In all, 54 divs were formed between 1 Nov 1942 and 8 Feb 1945. Initially 12 divs (4., 10. Croatia, 1.–4. Serbia, Herzegovina, Gorizia, Triglav, 3. Vojvodina, Kumanovo, Central Bosnia) had non-standard numbering and titles. However, by Oct 1944 all divs except Kumanovo had sequential numbers, military district and NO *(narodnooslobodilačka* – People's Liberation) titles. Three divs (numbered 1., 2. & 6.) received the highest distinction of 'Proletarian', while 31 (1.–4., 6.–11., 13., 14., 16., 17., 19.–22., 26., 27., 34.–38., 40., 42., 48., 51.–53.) were awarded the title 'Shock'.

Corps
On 9 Nov 1942, 1st Bosnia Corps was formed from 4. & 5. Divs, providing a strategic formation of about 5,000 personnel. A corps *(korpus)* had a flexible and frequently-changing organization, with 2–3 divs plus various ad hoc units. The first four corps, established 1942–43, were numbered and (except for 1st 'Proletarian' and 1st & 2nd 'Shock') bore the titles of the regions they were fighting in – 1st & 2nd Bosnia, 1st Croatia and 1st Slavonia/ 2nd Croatia. From Oct 1943, 16 of the 17 corps were numbered sequentially: 1st Proletarian, 2nd Shock, 3rd-16th, plus Bregalnica–Strumica.

Campaigns
The '4th Enemy Offensive' (Op *Weiß,*15 Jan–18 Mar 1943) was a major campaign. On 15 Jan Axis forces attacked 1st Croatian Corps, 6. Lika and 8. Kordun Divs in Lika, and 1st Bosnian Corps and 1. Prol Div in W Bosnia, but the Partisans escaped to Polkalinje on 18 February. The Axis captured the 'Bihać Republic' on 29 Jan, but 7. Banija Div and other Partisans stormed Chetnik defences on the Neretva river and escaped into E Bosnia, Herzegovina and Montenegro. The Axis plan to disarm the Chetniks

(Left) a Partisan *potporučnik* wearing M1943 officers' uniform with yellow metal collar triangles, and second-lieutenant's star-and-bar sleeve rank insignia. One of his men carries a British Bren LMG, and both are wearing the Yugoslav Army M1931 reversible shelter-quarter as a poncho – with (centre) splinter camouflage of light brown, dark brown and green on one side, and (right) plain field-grey or brown on the other. None of these men wears the red star badge on the M1942 *titovka* cap. (Museum of Yugoslavia, Belgrade)

(15–18 Mar) in case of an Allied landing was called off. In the '5th Enemy Offensive' (Op *Schwarz*,15 May–16 June), Axis forces attacked Partisans and Chetniks and encircled Mt Durmitor in N Montenegro, but 1. Prol Div's counterattack (21–27 May) preserved communication with E Bosnia. The 4. Montenegro, 7. Krajina and 10. Herzegovina Bdes then engaged Axis troops on Mt Bioč and the Piva river. On 4–9 June, Tito's GHQ was surrounded by German forces, but 1. Prol Div broke through the cordon at Zelengora, E Bosnia, then escaped across the Sutjeska river (10–15 June).

On 17 Sept 1943, the SOE officer Brig Fitzroy Maclean parachuted into Yugoslavia in Op 'Typical', leading a 13-strong British military mission ('Macmis') to the Partisans, including US Maj Linn 'Slim' Farish (OSS). Macmis organized delivery of substantial weaponry and supplies, and some supportive Allied air raids; a subsequent US military mission was led by Col Ellery Huntington Jr (OSS).

1944: Campaigns

The '6th Enemy Offensive' comprised three operations. In *Kugelblitz* (3 Dec 1943–Jan 1944), the Germans attacked Partisans in E and Central Bosnia; Op *Schneesturm* (21–29 Dec 1943) in Sandžak reduced Partisan territory, but failed to achieve decisive success. In Op *Herbstgewitter* (22 Dec 1943–15 Feb 1944), German forces defeated Partisans to occupy Korčula island, Dalmatia.

The '7th Enemy Offensive' (Op *Rösselsprung*, 25–27 May) involved a German SS airborne raid on Tito's GHQ in Drvar, W Bosnia, and converging ground advances by some 12,000 German and perhaps 6,000 Croatian and Chetnik forces. Thanks to bitter resistance by Partisan 1. Prol,, 8. and 5. Divs with Balkan Air Force support, Tito and his staff avoided capture, and transferred to Vis island under British protection.

On 16 July 1944 the 2,000-strong 1. Partisan Tank Bde formed, initially with 56 tanks supplied by the Allies, mainly US M3A3 Stuarts. They were organized in 1–3 (later 4) Tank Bns, each with one or two 3-ptn companies. An eng bn was formed, but not a planned armd car company.

Subsequent German operations in 1944 were led by 1. Gebirgs Div in Macedonia (the new Partisan designation for 'Vardar Macedonia'). In Op *Roeslein* (2 Aug), 13 Partisan divs entering Macedonia were forced back, and Op *Feuerwehr* (12 Aug) drove them from the Morava Valley. The Partisans retreated across the Lim river in the face of Op *Ruebezahl*, but still threatened German forces in E Macedonia.

On 8 Sept Bulgaria defected to the Allies, and troops immediately joined with Partisan 2., 5. and 17. Divs, but German forces held Skopje in Op *Treubruch* until 13 November. On 20 Oct Belgrade was captured by the Soviet Red Army and the so-called Partisan 1st Army Group *(Prva armiska grupa)* – formed early Oct with 1. Prol and 3. Montenegro Shock Divs, but dispersed after Belgrade. 2nd Army Group, formed 7 Dec 1944, was renamed Southern Operational Group *(Južna operativna grupa),* for operations in E Bosnia with 14th Corps, 17. and 28. Divisions.

Overseas Brigades

For service on the Adriatic islands and in Dalmatia and Bosnia, five of these (sing: *Prekomorska brigada)* were formed around Bari, SE Italy, from Slovene and Croatian POWs from the Italian Army.

The 1st Overseas Bde, formed 20 Oct 1943 at Carbonara di Bari, unsuccessfully resisted a German landing at Pelješac together with Partisan 13. Dalmatian and 2. Bde (7 Dec), and disbanded in Jan 1944. 2nd Overseas Bde, formed 7 Dec 1943, was disbanded at Drvar in Jan 1944, its personnel transferring to Partisan 1. and 6. Prol Divisions. 3rd Overseas Bde, formed 17 Dec 1943 at Gravina, landed at Brač; it liberated Bihać, Bosnia, on 28 Mar 1945, and Krk on 17 April. 4th Overseas Bde, formed at Gravina on 7 Sept 1943, was a labour unit until May 1945. 5th Overseas Bde was formed at Gravina in Sept 1944; it helped liberate Lika, Croatia, in Mar–Apr 1945, then Kočevo, Slovenia, and was disbanded on 20 April.

1945: Campaigns

By Jan 1945 the Partisans had evolved into a conventional army with considerable firepower, and Tito reorganized his now 800,000-strong forces. On 1 Jan three field Armies (numbered 1.–3.) were formed, followed on 1 Mar by 4. Army. These formations comprised 12 corps, 30 divs, and 6 independent brigades, and were collectively redesignated simply as the Yugoslav Army *(Jugoslovenska Armija* – JA). On 20 Mar 1945 the JA launched a general offensive northwards.

1. Army fought in Syrmia north of Belgrade, along with Soviet and Bulgarian troops; it broke through in mid-Apr, liberating N Slovenia, and reached Austria, where it fought Chetnik, Slovene and Croatian units on 13 March. Initially 2. Army fought in N Bosnia and liberated much of Central and W Bosnia, occupying Sarajevo and part of Croatia by 6 Apr; it captured Zagreb on 8 May and occupied Ljubljana, Slovenia, on 9 May. 3. Army occupied the Syrmian front Drava–Vukovar. In Apr it liberated N Croatia; in May it captured Maribor, Slovenia, defeating Axis forces at Poljana on 14–15 May.

4. Army was victorious in four operations: Mostar, Herzegovina (6–15 Feb); Lika-Primorje, Dalmatia and Istria (20 Mar–15 Apr); Rijeka (16 Apr–7 May); and Trieste (29 Apr–3 May), advancing into Carinthia, Austria. On 2 May, New Zealand 2nd Div of British 8 Army, advancing through NE Italy to Trieste, found that Yugoslav 4. Army had already occupied the city, claiming it for Tito. An uneasy truce ensued until 10 June, when both sides agreed to a partition line through the region. Trieste would only be fully returned to Italy in Oct 1954.

UNIFORMS & INSIGNIA
Caps & badges

Partisans initially wore various civilian clothing, or paramilitary and

Officers from 6.Vojvodina Bde HQ, January 1944. On the left is the OC *Vojvoda* Zarko Samardžić, wearing no rank insignia; on the right, Radonja Golubović displays on his left upper sleeve a red cloth chevron above a 5-point star, denoting his position as Deputy Brigade Commissar *(zamenik političkog komisara brigade).* Note that they too are not wearing red cap-stars. (Museum of Yugoslavia, Belgrade)

A Partisan field artillery battery from 8. Dalmatian Corps prepares to lay down barrage fire outside Knin, Southern Croatia, which was liberated on 9 December 1944. Note the US 75mm M1A1 pack howitzers on old M1 carriages with wooden wheels. (Museum of Yugoslavia, Belgrade)

military uniform items with coloured facings and badges removed.

A variety of caps included the greenish-grey cloth Slovene M1942 *triglavka* field cap (introduced 15 Apr 1942) with three 'peaks' along the crown seam; this was introduced in 1941 in Croatia as the *partizanka*, and in Dalmatia as the *troroga* from Nov 1941. There were four patterns: basic; with ear-flaps; with a peak; and with ear-flaps buttoned at the front. Other headgear included the M1942 *titovka* field cap (a copy of the Soviet *pilotka*), popular with HQ troops; the Serbian conical black fleece *šubara*; the white Albanian skull-cap, and the red Moslem fez. On 25 Apr 1944 Tito decreed that only the *titovka* should be worn.

The red metal or cloth 5-point cap star, introduced 4 July 1941, was prescribed for all military or civilian headgear. 'Proletarian' unit personnel from Feb 1942 wore a yellow cloth or metal hammer-and-sickle on the star. From 1 Oct 1941 different nationalities were also permitted a patch of their national tricolour flag on the cap, usually below the red star: Serbia, red (top)-blue-white; Croatia, red-white-blue; Slovenia, white-blue-red; Volunteer Dets, red-blue-white (no star). Other patterns were possible, including tricolour chevrons. The flag patches were abolished at the end of the war.

M1942 insignia
(see Chart 2, page 46)
From February 1942, command positions (rather than ranks) were indicated by red cloth stars and geometric shapes worn on the left upper sleeve of garments. The M1942a pattern (Feb–23 Sept 1942) had 9 positional titles and 7 badges (including Pte), and the M1942b pattern (24 Sept 1942–30 Apr 1943) had 28 titles and 18 badges. M1942 titles and M1943 ranks were written in the five languages recognized by Tito: Serbo–Croat, Serb, Croat, Slovene and Macedonian. (Chart 2 gives only the Serbian titles.)

M1943 uniforms & insignia
(see Chart 3, page 47)
During 1943 the Partisans developed a reasonably standard military uniform, although the mixture of captured enemy garments and military-style clothing manufactured by local factories inevitably produced a variety of styles and colours. Officers wore better-tailored items of superior quality.

Headgear (officers preferred the *titovka*) was as in 1941. The closed-collar tunic with shoulder straps (NCOs and enlisted men) or without (officers), had six front buttons, plain cuffs, and four external pockets with buttoned scalloped flaps. Officers wore riding breeches with leather riding or short-shaft marching boots; NCOs and men, German anklets and ankle boots. Officers wore a leather belt with cross-brace and holstered pistol, junior ranks a leather belt and combat equipment.

Conventional rank titles and insignia were introduced 21 May 1943. Officers and the warrant-officer rank wore gold metal six-point stars above braid bars on both cuffs, NCOs silver stars and cuff-bars. Officer rank groups wore yellow metal collar badges: general officers, diamonds with red underlay; field officers, diamonds; subaltern and warrant officers, triangles. Supreme HQ officers wore a gilt metal 5-point star on this collar badge.

M1944 uniforms & insignia

From 1944 many partisans wore British-supplied M1937 or M1940 khaki battledress or locally-made copies, with the *titovka* cap, anklets, ankle boots, and leather or webbing belts and rifle ammunition pouches. From 14 June 1944 'overseas' personnel in Italy could wear white or khaki drill summer uniforms.

In autumn 1944 new *titovka* badges were introduced. General officers wore a red enamel star edged in brass, on a 4–5cm 'sunrayed' oval cockade painted blue, above 2 small blue-over-silver chevrons points-up. Officers had a red star on a silver 33mm sunrayed cockade, and NCOs and enlisted men the star on a 28–31mm brass sunrayed cockade, both with the chevrons.

SELECT BIBLIOGRAPHY

Babac, Dušan M.: 'Vojne oznake y Srbiji 1845–1945' *(Military Badges in Serbia 1845–1945)* (Sluzbeni Glasnik, Belgrade, 2014)

Jevtić, Branko M.; 'Oznake Jugoslovenske Vojske i Otadzibini' *(Badges of the Yugoslav Army in the Homeland)* (CIP, Belgrade, 2011)

Mikulan, Krunoslav & Smutni, Emil, 'Partizanska vojska i Jugoslovenska armija 1941–1953' *(Partisan Army and Yugoslav Army 1941–1953)* (Despot Infinitus, Zagreb, 2016)

Švajncer, Janez J.: 'Uniforme' *(Uniforms)* (Muzej Novejse Zgodovine, Celje, 1997)

Vrišer, Sergej, 'Uniforme v Zgodovini: Slovenija in sosednje dezele' *(Uniforms in History : Slovenia and Neighbouring States)* (Partisan Books, Ljublana, 1987)

PLATE COMMENTARIES

A: YUGOSLAV ARMY, APRIL 1941

A1: *Kapetan I klase*, Infantry – Mechanized Battalion

This officer wears an M1939 *šajkača* field cap with dark red infantry piping, and M1939 officers' badge. The M1922 officer's greatcoat has branch-colour buttoned 'spearhead' collar patches; branch-colour edge-piping to the collar, front and cuffs; and shoulder straps of rank on branch-colour underlay, displaying the Mechanized Bn branch badge introduced July 1940 (see Chart 1, p.29, item 8). He wears an M1937 belt with a single cross-brace and the suspension strap for the M1939 dress dagger. His field equipment comprises an M1922 Adrian helmet, binoculars, and (obscured here) a holstered pistol and a mapcase.

A2: *Armijski djeneral*

The officer's M1939 peaked (visored) cap has light blue general officers' piping at the crown seam and band edges, and the M1939 officers' capbadge (though many generals preferred to wear the M1922 stiffened, peaked *šajkača*). The *dolman* undress jacket worn over his tunic has gold collar patches and light blue collar- and cuff-piping, with both sleeve- ranking and shoulder straps (see Chart 1, p.29, item 2). The M1922 officers' field tunic has a light blue standing collar; note the generals' 2 broad red seam-stripes on the breeches, and the gold-braided *šajkača* tucked under his belt, which he wears with both support straps. At his throat, note the Order of the White Eagle with Swords.

A3: *Kaplar*, Infantry

This lance-corporal wears an Adrian helmet in greenish-grey with a Yugoslav frontal plate. His greenish-grey M1924 *koporan* field tunic shows large branch-colour collar patches, and the single silver rank-star on the shoulder straps. His matching trousers are worn with puttees and ankle boots. He carries M1924 field equipment with 2 rifle ammunition pouches on the M1933 belt, a slung M1924 waterbottle, and (obscured here) the M1924 'breadbag' haversack and M1927 gasmask. The standard rifle was

43

initially the M1924 7.92mm Mauser made by FN Herstal, but later the virtually identical 'M24' licence-built at the Kragujevac arsenal.

B: YUGOSLAV ARMY, APRIL 1941
B1: *Podnarednik,* 3rd Battalion, 1st Mountain Infantry Regt
This corporal wears the M1922 *šajkača* with M1934 NCO cockade. His M1932 mountain tunic, with 4 external pockets and horizontal cuff-flaps, has infantry collar patches with a brass battalion number and a silver NCOs' button, and shoulder straps with the brass horn branch badge (but no regimental number in wartime). On his right breast is the coloured enamel mountain qualification badge, and on both sleeves 2 M1932 yellow rank chevrons. He has windproof 'plus-four' trousers, long and short socks and climbing boots. A cloak hangs from a back-strap over the same field equipment as A3, and note skis and ski-sticks.

B2: *Redov,* Guards Cavalry Brigade
The Royal Guards Brigade was the first of very few units to receive the M1934 Czechoslovak *Čačak* helmet. This trooper in field dress wears the M1924 Guards tunic; the apparently all- light blue collar actually bears large L-shaped light blue braids. Note the gilt toggle buttons, narrow gold-cord

Djeneralštabni Major (Staff Maj) Ivo Fregl, wearing the M1939 uniform with officers' badge on his *šajkača* field cap. He displays M1939 staff *aiguillettes,* and (just visible on his right breast pocket) the silver badge of a graduate of the Military Academy senior course; on his left breast is the Soldier's Merit Medal. Although a Slovene, Fregl was committed to the Chetniks. When he was shot by German forces in Valjevo, Serbia, on 16 December 1944, his last wish was to give the orders to the firing squad that executed him. (Courtesy Fregl family)

shoulder straps bearing Aleksandar I's monogram, and dark green piping including cuff-knots. He wears field breeches and spurred riding boots with gilt rosettes at the upper front; note the Guards M1899 ammunition pouch, and .32in M1922 Belgian FN Browning pistol. The machine gun is an 8mm Austrian M1907/12 Schwarzlose.

B3: *Narednik Vodnik III Klase,* Anti-Aircraft Artillery
This WO 3rd Class wears an M1939 *šajkaca,* with an M1939 NCOs' double-headed eagle badge in silver on branch-colour backing. The M1939 enlisted men's tunic has artillery-black collar patches and piping, and the AA branch badge on M1939 tunic-colour shoulder straps. Note the knee-length leather gaiters, and the belt with cross-brace supporting a Browning pistol and binoculars.

C YUGOSLAV ARMY, APRIL 1941
C1: *Poručnik,* 1st Tank Battalion
This lieutenant wears a French M1919 tank helmet, light grey summer overalls with a rank patch above the left breast pocket, and ankle boots. Some tank crews wore locally-made reinforced leather helmets.

C2: *Narednik,* Chetnik Assault Battalion, 1st Army
This sergeant wears an M1939 sheepskin *kalpak* with a black tasselled bag and NCOs' capbadge. The M1940 'assault tunic', is as B1, but with black piping, and black collar patches with silver death's-head branch badges. His cape has collar patches, and 3 black rank bars on the left breast. His belt supports a Browning pistol and an M1924 ČK dagger-shaped bayonet for the assault carbine.

C3: *Potporučnik,* 1st Parachute Company
This Air Force company, formed in March 1940, used American Irvin backpack parachutes produced in Yugoslavia under licence; they practised accelerated jumps in free fall without a static line, but saw no action in the April War. This second-lieutenant wears a leather helmet produced locally by Knebl & Dietrich, and a greyish-green canvas tank overall with a gold braid rank bar on grey-blue backing on the left breast pocket. The revolver is an Austrian 8mm M1898 Rast Gasser.

C3a: Parachute qualification badge
This gold and silver badge depicts a Serbian crown, a Yugoslav coat of arms, and an eagle clutching a rifle; it was worn on the right breast pocket of the Air Force M1937 greyish-blue service tunic.

D: ROYAL YUGOSLAV FORCES, 1942–44
D1: *Narednik Vodnik II Klase,* Royal Guards Bn; Halfaya Pass, March 1942
This warrant officer wears British Army khaki-drill field uniform with the officer's service-dress cap, which bears an M1939 Yugoslav NCOs' capbadge on dark red infantry backing. His shirt displays 2 gold-on- black rank bars as shoulder-strap slides, and the red eagle shoulder patch of 4th Indian Division. His webbing equipment is officers' 1937 Pattern, and he carries a 38in Enfield No 2 Mk 1 revolver.

D2: *Podnarednik,* 10 (Interallied) Commando; Vis Island, February 1944
This corporal of the unit's small No.7 (Yugoslav) Troop wears the same capbadge as D1 on his green M1942 Commando beret. Sewn to the heavy khaki woollen sweater worn over his KD shirt are the red-on-khaki M1942 'YUGOSLAVIA' title above the red-on-blue 'N° 10 COMMANDO', the Combined Operations badge, and British rank chevrons. His primary

weapon is the M1928A1 Thompson sub-machine gun, and his webbing includes 2 'basic' ammunition pouches. Note also the 'toggle-rope' around his waist, and the M1941 Fairbairn-Sykes Commando knife.

D3: Brigadier Charles Armstrong; British SOE liaison mission to Gen Mihailović, April 1944

Armstrong was Mihailović 's last BLO (Oct 1943–May 1944). His service-dress cap and battledress show the red band and gorget patches and the capbadge of a staff officer; his shoulder straps bear the embroidered crown and 3 'pips' of his rank. He chooses to wear his M1940 parachute wings on his left breast above the ribbons of the Military Cross (awarded for gallantry in North Russia,1919), and the Distinguished Service Order (awarded for his command of 1/6th Bn, East Surrey Regt with the BEF in France,1940).

E: YUGOSLAV ARMY IN THE HOMELAND, 1941–45

E1: *Narednik* Bozidar Perović, Supreme Command; Bosnia, 1942

Sergeant Perović held the position of Supreme Command standard-bearer, carrying the flag of the 41st Inf Regt (one of the few not captured in April 1941). His *kalpak* bears the M1939 NCOs' badge. He wears a Yugoslav officer's *dolman,* without insignia, over a British battledress blouse, Yugoslav breeches. puttees, and mountain socks and boots. He is armed with a Thompson SMG, a Browning pistol, an officer's dagger, and M1935 grenades.

E2: *Armijski djeneral* Dragoljub Mihailović; Serbia, August 1944

In 1941, Col Mihailović had been a 2. Army staff officer, known for his outspoken criticism of the Supreme Command. Here he wears a *šajkača* cap with a general officer's badge, and an M1932 mountain cape with infantry collar patches and piping, over British battledress, leather jerkin, anklets and boots. He carries a 9mm Walther P38 pistol and a .30cal US M1 carbine. Insignia obscured here included silver USAAF pilot's wings above the left breast pocket, presented in August 1944 in appreciation for rescuing US aircrew; and an unofficial left-sleeve patch with an eagle and '*Svome čika Draži – jarušičanke*' ('To our uncle Draža – from the women of Janus'), probably presented by factory-workers supplying the Chetniks.

E3: *Major* Predrag Raković, 2nd Ravna Gora Corps; Serbia, 1944

Raković commanded the élite 2nd Ravna Gora Corps. He wears a *šajkača* with M1939 badge, and items of traditional Serbian folk dress: a heavily embroidered *anterija* jacket worn over a German Panzer shirt, grey breeches, long dark brown socks, and brown leather *opanci* sandals. On his left forearm only, note the narrow-over-wide gold diagonal bars of the April 1944 rank insignia. He carries a German 9mm MP40 SMG with one set of magazine pouches, a holstered P38, and the M1924 bayonet issued to 1940 Chetnik assault units.

F: CHETNIKS & PARTISAN DETACHMENTS, 1941–42

F1: *Borac,* National Liberation Partisan Detachments of Yugoslavia; Serbia, July 1941

This 'fighter' wears a *šajkača* without a red star badge, either because he is a non-Communist UNOF guerilla, or because he is heeding Moscow's instructions to play down Soviet influence. He has a modified M1939 tunic, black civilian breeches, long black woollen socks with peasant floral

Following the Soviet example, many women volunteered for service with the Partisans. These three all rank as *zastavnik* (warrant officer), wearing various privately-purchased tunics with subaltern officers' yellow-metal collar triangles, and single gold braid rank bars on their sleeves. Note that they all wear red cap-stars, and the officers' service belt. (Dušan Babac Collection)

decoration, and *opanci* shoes. He wears a German belt and brown ammunition pouches, and carries Yugoslav grenades, an M1924 rifle, and a 7.63mm C96-series Mauser 'broomhandle' pistol in its wooden holster-stock.

F2: *Vojvoda* Momčilo Djujić; Lika, 1942

The Chetnik commander of the Dinara (Coastal) Div in N Dalmatia and W Bosnia, this former Orthodox priest wears a Serbian *šubara* conical lambswool cap, with the prewar Chetnik Association badge of a double-headed eagle with crossed bayonets and death's-head. His privately-tailored tunic has silver buttons, and a turn-down collar piped black, with black 'spearhead' patches (sometimes bearing the silver skull-and-crossbones). His weapons are a Browning pistol and an Italian 9mm Beretta MP38 SMG. One of very few *vojvode* to avoid British repatriation to the Partisans after surrender, Djujić was unique among them in reaching exile in the USA, dying in 1999 in San Diego at the age of 92.

F3: *Komandant bataljona*, Partisan 'Velebit' Detachment; Lika, March 1942

This Croatian senior captain wears the *triglavka* variant of the *partizanka* cap, rising to three 'peaks' along the crown, and with the red star badge. His Italian M1934 leather coat bears M1942 Partisan rank insignia on the left sleeve (see Chart 2, item 11). His weapons and greenish-grey belts are also Italian: a holstered 7.65mm M1935 Beretta pistol, a 6.5mm M1891 Carcano carbine, and the mounted troops' pouch-bandolier.

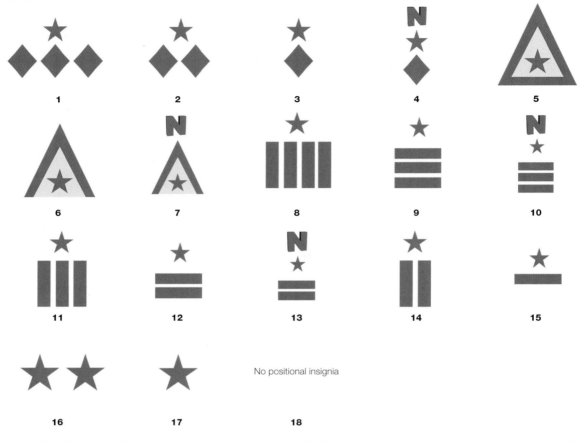

1   2   3   4   5

6   7   8   9   10

11   12   13   14   15

No positional insignia

16   17   18

Key: Positional titles in latinized Serbian, followed by:
(English translation) – British Army equivalent.
Insignia worn in red on left sleeve of all tunics and greatcoats.
1st pattern insignia (identified by asterisks) were introduced in February 1942, and replaced by 2nd pattern (without asterisks) from 24 Sept 1942.

(1–4) General officer equivalents; (5–15) officers; (16–18) NCOs and enlisted men.

1: *Komandant glavnog štaba* (Chief of General Staff) – Gen
2: *Komandant operativne zone* (Commander of Operational Zone) – MajGen
3: *Zamenik komandanta glavnog štaba* (Deputy Chief of General Staff) / *Zamenik komandant operativne zone* (Deputy Cdr of OZ) –Brigadier
4: *Načelnik štaba operativne zone* (Chief of Staff of OZ) – Brigadier
5: *Komandant brigade* (Brigade Commander) / *Komandant grupe odreda* (Cdr of Group of Detachments) – Brigadier
6: *Zamenik komandanta brigade* (Deputy Brigade Commander) / *Zamenik komandanat grupe odreda* (Deputy Cdr of Grp of Detachments) – Colonel

6*: *Komandant brigade* (Brigade Cdr) / *Komandant grupe odreda* (Cdr of Grp of Detachments) – Colonel
7: *Načelnik štaba brigade* (Chief of Bde Staff) / *Načelnik štaba grupe odreda* (Chief of Staff of Group of Detachments) – Colonel
8: *Komandant odreda* (Detachment Commander) – Lieutenant-Colonel
9: *Zamenik komandanta odreda* (Deputy Detachment Cdr) – Major
9*: *Komandant odreda* (Detachment Cdr) – Lieutenant-Colonel
10: *Načelnik staba odreda* (Det Chief of Staff) – Major
11: *Komandant bataljona* (Battalion Commander) – (Senior Captain)
12: *Zamenik komandanta bataljona* (Deputy Bn Cdr) – Captain
12*: *Komandant bataljona* (Bn Cdr) – (Senior Capt)
13: *Načelnik staba bataljona* (Chief of Bn Staff) – Captain
14: *Komandir četa* (Company Commander) – Lieutenant
15: *Zamenik komandira čete* (Deputy Co Cdr) – 2nd Lieutenant
15*: *Komandir četa* (Co Cdr) – Lieutenant
16* & 16: *Vodnik* (Platoon Commander) – Sergeant
17* & 17: *Desetar* (Section Commander) – Corporal
18* & 18: *Borac* ('Fighter') – Private

G: NATIONAL LIBERATION PARTISAN DETACHMENTS, 1943–44
G1: *Vodnik;* Slovenia, December 1943
This Slovene sergeant wears a peaked field cap with buttoned-up ear-flaps, displaying a red star above a white-blue-red Slovenian flag patch. He displays two red rank stars on the left sleeve of an Italian M1940 field tunic, with breeches, puttees, turn-down socks and climbing boots. He holds a 7.9mm Zbrojovkla M1937 light machine gun. His equipment includes San Giorgio 8 x 30 binoculars, a Yugoslav M1935 belt with double Italian M1936 rifle ammunition pouches supported by a neck strap, and a Browning pistol. Three smooth-cased Yugoslav M1938 'offensive' concussion grenades hang from a cross strap, and segmented M1935 'defensive' fragmentation grenades at his waist.

G2: *Borac,* 2nd Proletarian Brigade; March 1943
This 15-year-old courier wears a grey M1942 *titovka* cap with

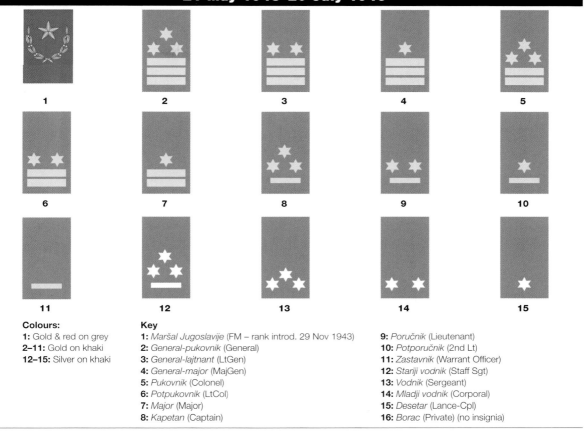

Colours:
1: Gold & red on grey
2–11: Gold on khaki
12–15: Silver on khaki

Key
1: *Maršal Jugoslavije* (FM – rank introd. 29 Nov 1943)
2: *General-pukovnik* (General)
3: *General-lajtnant* (LtGen)
4: *General-major* (MajGen)
5: *Pukovnik* (Colonel)
6: *Potpukovnik* (LtCol)
7: *Major* (Major)
8: *Kapetan* (Captain)
9: *Poručnik* (Lieutenant)
10: *Potporučnik* (2nd Lt)
11: *Zastavnik* (Warrant Officer)
12: *Stariji vodnik* (Staff Sgt)
13: *Vodnik* (Sergeant)
14: *Mladji vodnik* (Corporal)
15: *Desetar* (Lance-Cpl)
16: *Borac* (Private) (no insignia)

the 'Proletarian' unit badge, and a Hungarian M1920 greatcoat. He carries messages along with his small kit in an M1924 'breadbag'; a waterbottle; and an apparently cut-down British M1942 'bandolier, Sten', originally with seven magazine pockets.

G3: *General-lajtnant* Peko Dapcević; Belgrade, October 1944
Dapcević commanded 1st Proletarian Corps, which liberated the Yugoslav capital on 20 October 1944. He wears a grey uniform with the M1944 general officers' badge on the *titovka* cap. The tunic has a general's gold metal diamond collar badges edged red, bearing a gold star, and on both forearms May 1943 rank insignia of 2 gold stars above 3 gold bars (see Chart 3, item 3). His decorations (left to right) are the Order of the Partisan Star 1st Class; the Soviet Order of Suvorov 2nd Class; and the Partisan Commemorative Medal.

H: NATIONAL LIBERATION ARMY, 1944–45
H1: *Potporučnik,* 1st Tank Brigade; Šibenik, October 1944
This Stuart tank platoon commander in the Partisans' élite spearhead force wears a British M1941 black leather 'crash helmet, Royal Armoured Corps' with a red-painted star. A May 1943 star-and-bar second-lieutenant's rank badge is worn below the deep left breast pocket of the British M1943 'oversuit, tank crews'; this 'pixie suit' has its outsize blanket-lined hood opened over his shoulders. His sidearm is

an Enfield No 2 Mark 1* revolver in an M1941 'case, pistol, web, Royal Armoured Corps' on leg straps.

H2: *Maršal Jugoslavije* Tito, October 1944
Marshal Tito wore gold-thread rank insignia on his uniforms from 29 November 1943. Two patterns of insignia were worn during 1943–45, and this dark blueish-grey uniform displays elements of both. The M1944 peaked cap has gold-embroidered laurel branches and a gold metal badge on a red band above a gold-lace strap. The first-pattern 5-leaf laurel branch collar insignia were worn on grey patches, but this second pattern on red patches. This first-pattern sleeve insignia is 2 laurel branches forming a wreath with a 5-point star at the apex, while the second pattern had a 'horseshoe' shape, with the star in the centre (see Chart 3, item 1). His breeches have 2 wide red stripes divided by the outseam. He wears a Red Army officer's M1935 brown leather belt with a 'star' buckle.

H3: *Stariji vodnik,* 4th Army; Trieste, May 1945
This staff sergeant wears an M1942 khaki *titovka*, and British M1940 battledress introduced in 1942, with May 1943 ranking of 3 silver stars and a bar on khaki sleeve patches. He carries a 7.62mm Soviet PPSh-41 sub-machine gun with a late 'banana' magazine, but still has an M1941 pouch for the old 'drum' magazine on his belt.

INDEX